THE
TEMPLARS'
CAMINO

A Guidebook to the Knights Templar
on the Camino de Santiago

BRIAN JOHN SKILLEN

Published by: Publishing Hackers
Arvada, Colorado, USA

ISBN Paperback: 978-1-959911-39-5
ISBN Hardcover: 978-1-959911-44-9
ISBN Ebook: 978-1-959911-43-2

Design and formatting by Publishing Hackers
Image Credits: Víctor Badia Calvet, Wiesiek Zienkiewicz, José Luis San Juan España, C. L. Morales, and Wikicommons
Maps provided by: https://www.gronze.com/

You can contact Brian at Brian@brianjohnskillen.com

Thank you

No quest is ever taken alone. I would like to thank Stephan Viollier, Víctor Badia Calvet, Mariesol, José Luis San Juan España, Saturnino Blanco García, El Camino People, Juan Carlos Flórez Álvarez, Marta Manuela Fernández San Juan, Charo Fernández Rodríguez, José Rodríguez Valín, Manuel Colinas Bodelón, and Wiesiek Zienkiewicz, who walked the miles with me, endured trials, and helped me to translate when I didn't understand. It is thanks to them that this book is what it is. Also, a special thank you to my Beta Readers, Michelle Skillen, and Malina Dravis-Tucker.

Heredero del único cielo,
Vuelve el valiente cruzado
del sol, el rostro tostado
y tinto Rioja en acero.

Y las lunas dominadas,
de los infieles cautivos,
Mil caballos, mil victorias,
mil cimitarras ganadas

Las ocas

Boyzzon
25-7-2
www.arteenreformas.es

Heir of the only Heaven,
the brave crusader returns,
of the sun, the tanned face
and red Rioja on his steel.

And the dominated Moons,
of the captive infidels,
A thousand horses, a thousand victories,
a thousand earned swords.

The Geese

This book is for adventurers, those who have dreamt of knights, distant lands, and their very own Grail quest.

TABLE OF CONTENTS

Introduction. 1

Day 1: Somport to Jaca | 32 km. 7

Day 2: Jaca & Arres | 39.4 km. 11

Day 3: Arres to Ruesta | 27.4 km. 16

Day 4: Ruesta to Sangüesa | 22 km 19

Day 5: Sangüesa – Monreal | 27.2 km 23

Day 6: Monreal – Puente la Reina | 31 km 26

Day 7: Puenta la Reina to Estella | 21.6 km 30

Day 8: Estella – Los Arcos | 21.3 km 33

Day 9: Los Arcos – Logroño | 27.6 km. 35

Day 10: Logroño – Nájera | 29 km 39

Day 11: Nájera to Santo Domingo de
Calzada | 20.7 km 42

Day 12: Santo Domingo de la Calzada to
Belorado | 21.8 km. 46

Day 13: Belorado to San Juan de Ortega | 23.9 km 48

Day 14: San Juan de Ortega to Burgos | 25.8 km. 51

Day 15: Burgos to The Arc of San Anton | 39 km 56

Day 16: Castrojeriz | 3.9 km Rest day 60

Day 17: Castrojeriz to Fromista | 24.7 km 65

Day 18: Formista to Carrión de los Condes | 18.8 km . .67

Day 19: Carrión de los Condes to
Terradillos de los Templarios | 26.3 km 70

Day 20: Terradillos de los Templarios to
Mansilla de las Mulas | 53 km 74

Day 21: Mansilla de las Mulas to León | 18.5 km 76

Day 22: León to Hospital de Órbigo | 31.44 km 80

Day 23: Hospital de Órbigo to Astorga | 15.3 km 83

Day 24: Astorga to Foncebadón | 28.5 km 85

Day 25: Foncebadón to
Espinoso de Compludo | 22 km 87

Day 26: Espinoso de Compludo to
Ponferrada | 14.6 km 90

Day 27: Ponferrada to Las Médulas | 27.8 km 94

Day 28: Las Médulas to
O' Barco de Valdeorras | 27.2 km 98

Day 29: O Barco de Valdeorras to Quiroga | 38.5 km . 102

Day 30: Quiroga to Monforte de Lemos | 35.4 km . . . 104

Day 31: Monfort de Lemos to chantada | 30.4 km 107

Day 32: Chantada to Roderio | 25.4 km 109

Day 33: Roderio to Silleda | 37.6 km 111

Day 34: Silleda to Santiago de Compostela | 40.6 km . 113

Other Books By Brian John Skillen
about the Camino de Santiago 118

Bibliography 120

About the Author 121

INTRODUCTION

In the shadow of the Medieval World, where battles and faith carved the map of Europe, stands a monumental testament to a journey of spiritual discovery and historical intrigue: the Camino de Santiago. This book unfolds the layers of a narrative that began with the Battle of Covadonga in 722. This pivotal clash marked the dawn of the Christian Kingdom of Asturias, setting the stage for the reconquest of the Iberian Peninsula, a land fragmented by conflict yet bound by a quest for spiritual enlightenment and unity.

Under the reign of King Alfonso II, this young kingdom was woven with the threads of faith, ambition, and diplomacy. Recognized by the likes of Charlemagne and the Pope, Alfonso II's conquests and reign fostered a bridge between the isolated Asturias and the broader Carolingian lands. However, it was the divine declaration of the discovery of St. James the Great's holy bones in Galicia that heralded a new era. This revelation transformed Santiago de Compostela into a beacon for pilgrims across Europe, igniting the Camino de Santiago, a pilgrimage that transcended mere physical boundaries to become a route of spiritual significance.

The legend of Saint James and the miraculous discovery of his tomb create a narrative that challenges the historical and the mystical. The Camino de Santiago, rooted in these tales of celestial phenomena and divine intervention, emerged as not only a path to the sacred but also as a conduit for cultural, political, and spiritual exchange. The establishment of the pilgrimage route, from its inception to its architectural embodiment in the Cathedral of Santiago de Compostela, encapsulates a journey through time, faith, and the quest for understanding.

Through the subsequent centuries, the Kingdom of Asturias fragmented into the kingdoms of Aragon, Navarra, Castilia, Leon, Galacia, and Portugal, each playing its part in medieval geopolitics and the expansion of the Camino de Santiago.

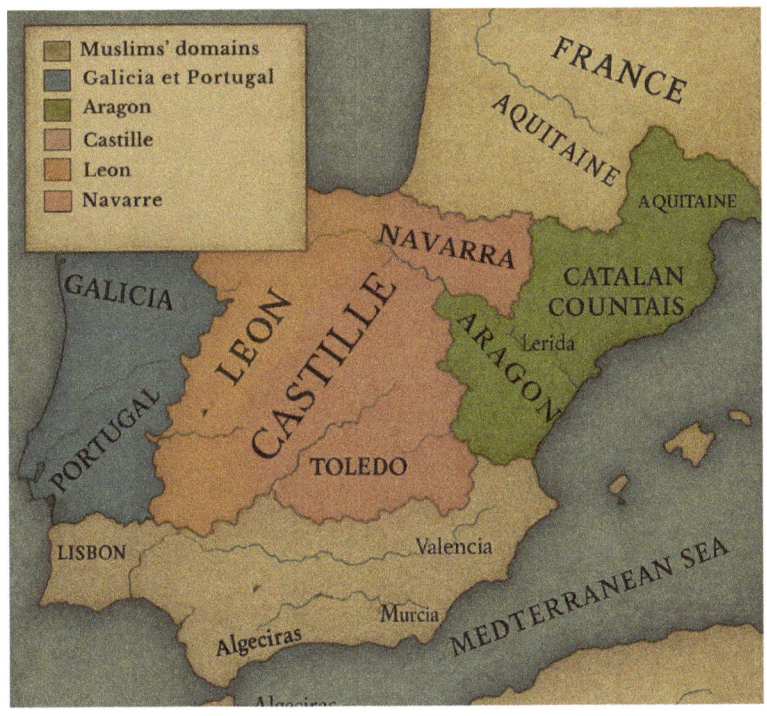

The Templars' Camino, invites you to traverse this ancient path, exploring the interwoven destinies of kingdoms, the spiritual fervor that propelled thousands to undertake this journey, and the presence of the Knights Templar—a mysterious military order founded in Jerusalem sworn to the protection of pilgrims. Their legacy is etched into the very stone of the pilgrimage itself and their swords helped to forge the realm. The Templars' legacy is bound in great treasure, spiritual relics, and a mysterious disappearance of both. Could the Camino de Santiago hold the secrets that have eluded researchers for years?

The Templars' Camino is a compilation of four different routes on the Camino de Santiago: the Aragonese Camino, Frances, Iverno, and Via de la Plata. Combined, these paths show you the most interesting Templar sites the Camino has to offer. Your journey starts in Somport, France, and ends in Santiago de Compostela, where the body of St. James is said to rest. It will take you through five different kingdoms of Medieval Spain and guide you to discover the secrets the Templars left behind.

All maps in this guidebook were provided by www.gronze.com I recommend that you download their app for your journey.

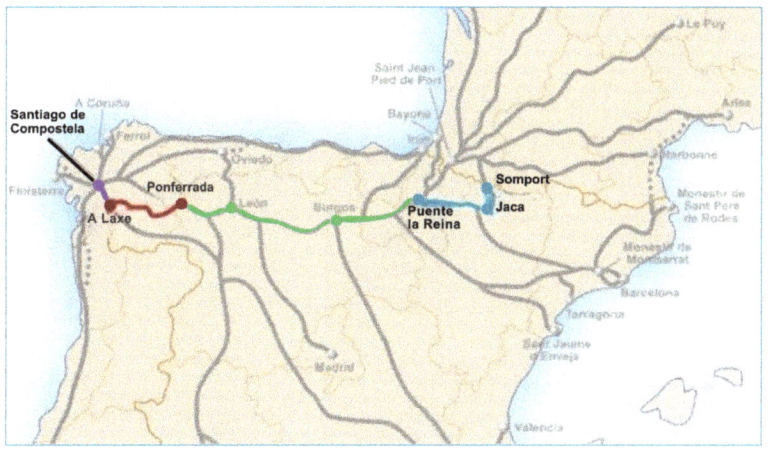

Download your Camino de Santiago Packing List

https://books.brianjohnskillen.com/CaminodeSantiagoPackingList

KINGDOM OF

ARAGON

DAY 1:

SOMPORT TO JACA | 32 KM

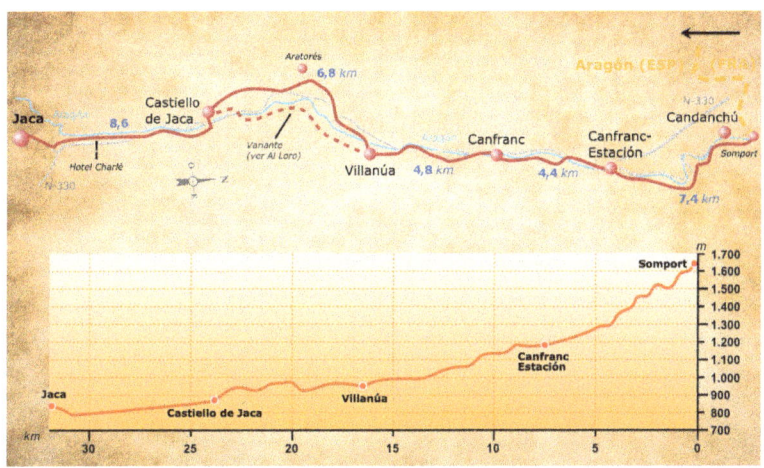

Dear adventurer, welcome to your quest to find the Knights Templar on the Camino de Santiago. Day one of our journey will take us from Somport to Jaca, a distance of 32 km, on the Aragonese Camino.

We are starting our journey on the Aragonese Camino because the Kingdom of Aragon was a hotbed for Templars throughout the Middle Ages. The Templars owned vast properties in the Kingdom of Aragon and were integrated with the monarchy, but we will talk more about that later.

The day before you begin your Camino, I recommend that you take the bus from Jaca to Canfranc. Here, you will find a modern albergue (pilgrims' hostel) with all of the amenities.

The descent from Somport to Canfranc is one of the steepest out of all of the Caminos. So prepare yourself for a good hike tomorrow and take precautions to save your knees for the rest of the journey.

In the morning, you can catch the 8:50 bus from Canfranc to Somport, which is right on the French border. Here, you officially begin your Templars' Camino by getting the first stamp in your Pilgrim's Passport, also known as a Credential. This seemingly simple document ties you into a tradition stretching back to the Templars and their innovative approach to safeguarding pilgrims and their wealth.

Your Camino Credential is not just a record-keeping document. It carries echoes of a time when the Knights Templar acted as financial custodians for pilgrims. In the medieval era, pilgrims would store their gold with their local Templar commandery and receive a coded credential that they could use much like an ATM card to withdraw funds at strategically placed Templar commanderies on their pilgrimage route. Today, as you use this document, you inherit that tradition.

The only word I have to describe the Aragonese Comino is majestic. As you make your descent from Somport, cliffs tower on either side of you, and the mist clings to the mountains until the sun breaks through. The Camino follows the Aragon River down. Its rushing waters bubble at your side as you walk. It is easy to imagine yourself transported back in time as a Templar coming to this country from the Holy Land. Granted, the Pope forbade the Kingdoms on the Iberian Peninsula from sending their soldiers to the Crusades. They were to remain for the reconquest of Spain from the Moors. After the fall of Jerusalem, however, many of the Knights from the Holy Land came

to the Iberian Peninsula for the Reconquista and also to protect pilgrims along the pilgrimage routes.

On your way down the mountain, make sure to stop at Canfranc Estación to admire what was once one of the most beautiful train stations in Europe and has now been converted into a hotel. It is also a great place to fill up your water bottle, as there are several fountains in town. From here, you will find a giant dam as well as a waterfall, which are just spectacular. Take a moment and admire the beauty and the power of nature.

Next, you pass through Canfranc. Here, you can pick up your bag if you left it behind and continue on for another 20.2 km to Jaca, where we will stay for the night and prepare for our journey to San Juan de la Pena, where we encounter our first Holy Grail legend.

DAY 2:
JACA & ARRES | 39.4 KM

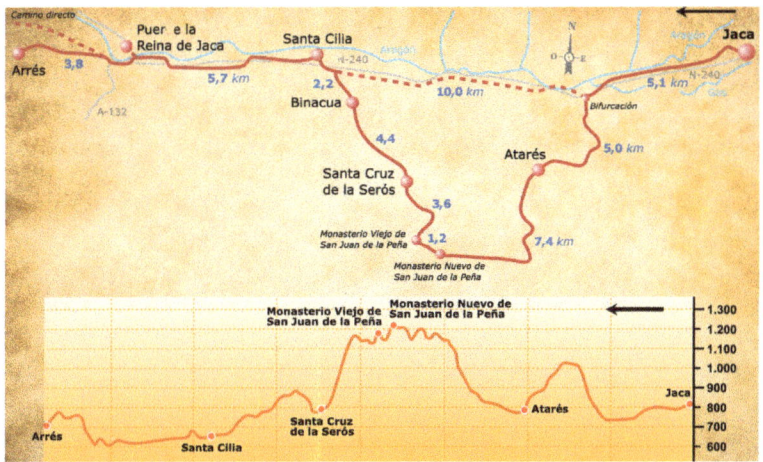

The Holy Grail has always been synonymous with the Knights Templar. So, I thought, what better place to start our quest to find the Templars on the Camino than the Monastery of San Juan de la Peña, where the Holy Grail was once kept?

Leaving Jaca, you have two options: the first route will take you directly to Arrés, which is 24.6 km away. But our adventure takes us on the alternative route, leading to the Monastery of San Juan de la Peña. Legend has it that the monastery once housed the Holy Grail. The story goes that the Holy Grail was included on an inventory list found in the monastery. This grail was lost and found several times and is now believed to be in the Cathedral of Valencia.

Another interesting fact is that the Kings of Aragon were also buried at San Juan de la Peña, which raises the question: was the Holy Grail stored here truly a cup, or was it a bloodline?

The hike from Jaca to the New Monastery of San Juan de la Peña takes you from one mesa to another. It is a breathtaking climb on beautiful paths. To reach the monastery, you must climb nearly 500 meters, with a sharp descent on the other side.

The new monastery is only 17.5 km from Jaca. If you are splitting the 39 km day in two, you can stay here for the evening at a hotel and spend the day exploring. If you continue, I recommend skipping the New Monastery and heading straight to the Old Monastery. This structure is one of the most striking sights on the Camino. The medieval monastery is built into the side of the mountain, with a sheer rock face hanging above it like Damocles' sword.

As you step inside the monastery, you step back in time. Your journey begins in the lower cloister. Take your time and explore. To the left of the two chapels, you will find a goose-foot symbol carved into the stone. This symbol will become central to our search for the Templars on the Camino but will be discussed in a later chapter.

After you have finished exploring, ascend the stairs to an open courtyard. On the left wall, you will see several carvings, including Templar crosses. After you have explored the courtyard, continue into the main chapel. On the left, you will see three alcove chapels. The center one contains a replica of the Holy Grail that was believed to have been housed here.

Next, continue through the chapel to another open court-yard, where you will find a magnificent cloister of pillars. Each pillar has a story carved into it. The most interesting one is the pillar that depicts the Last Supper. In this image, there are several interesting details. Firstly, it looks as if Jesus is holding a finger to the lips of the person to his right while pointing at him. Secondly, in front of Jesus rests a fish, not bread. Thirdly, the person to Jesus' left is cuddled up to him, holding what could be interpreted as a bundle of joy. This image was created in the 12th century, many years before Da Vinci painted his rendition of the Last Supper.

Conclude your journey at San Juan de la Peña at the Royal Pantheon, where the kings of Aragon were laid to rest. The most interesting King of Aragon, in regard to the Templars, Alfonso the Battler, isn't buried here, but we will speak more about him later. I will say this, though: He was supposedly the keeper of the Holy Grail, which gives credence to the belief that the Grail was once stored in this magnificent structure.

After you visit the monastery, prepare for the 19.7 km walk to Arrés. It is a steep downhill descent from the monastery, then mostly flat until the final ascent to Arrés. When you arrive, enjoy the sunset, and I recommend staying at the donativo Albergue de Peregrinos de Arrés. Here, you will enjoy a communal meal with fellow adventurers, meeting your companions for the coming days.

DAY 3:
ARRES TO RUESTA | 27.4 KM

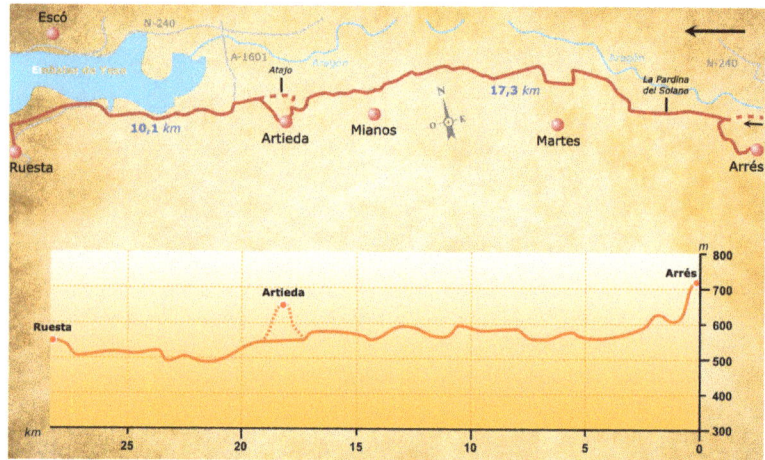

My fellow adventurer, I invite you to continue your journey to Ruesta, 27.4 km away. From Arrés, it is a gentle downhill descent until you get to Artieda. Here, you have the option to bypass the town or climb the 100 meters to the top. For our Templar Journey, I recommend climbing to the top for two reasons. Firstly, there is a nice albergue with good food and an amazing view. Secondly, all of the street signs you see will have the Seed of Life on them.

The Seed of Life is one of the building blocks of sacred geometry. It consists of seven interconnected circles that create the image of a six-petaled shape. It is said that each of the circles that form the Seed of Life represents a day of creation. This symbol is found all around the world and is associated with Kabbalah, a form of Jewish mysticism. The Seed of Life is often found in close proximity to Templar sites. It is said that when the Templars were in the Holy Land, they exchanged information with many cultures and learned many hidden secrets.

From Artieda, it is a 10 km walk to Ruesta. The journey takes you through a forest and close to the lake of Embalsa de Yesa.

As you approach Ruesta, the first thing you see is a giant castle with two spires surrounded by a dilapidated city. Entering the abandoned city, you pass a cathedral that has been chained up and abandoned to time. These ruins whisper of the Templars through their very architecture itself. The inner temple of the cathedral is shaped like an octagon, a characteristic feature of many Templar churches across Europe. This design mimics the layout of the Templars' headquarters in Jerusalem. We will be exploring several of these octagonal churches in the coming days and discussing why the Templars used this unique design. Enjoy your stay at the albergue in Ruesta, it is the only habitation left in this forgotten city.

DAY 4:
Ruesta to Sangüesa | 22 km

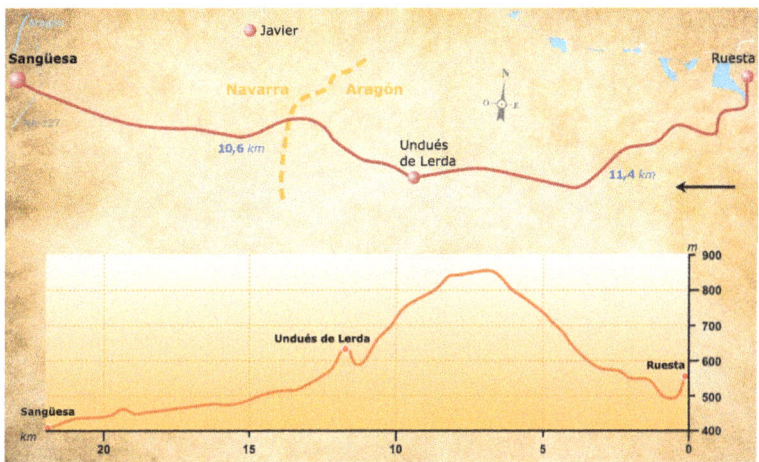

After your restful night's sleep in the abandoned town, continue your journey to Sangüesa, which is 22 km away. As you leave town, make sure to take a moment to look back and admire the castle. This site will transport you back in time. Imagine yourself a knight, looking back as he must continue on.

About fifteen minutes after you leave Ruesta, a small chapel will appear on your left. Inside, you will find three stone carvings. The first has a Templar cross carved into it, the second a Seed of Life, and the third has been lost to time. This chapel is further evidence that the Templars were present in this part of the land.

Three-quarters of the way through your journey, you will pass from Aragon to Navarra. These provinces in Spain were once powerful kingdoms that can trace their roots back to 722 CE and the Battle of Covadonga. This clash marked the dawn of the Christian Kingdom of Asturias, setting the stage for the Reconquest of Spain from the Moors.

Most people know about the Crusades in the Holy Land, but they often don't know that the Reconquest of Spain was also deemed a Crusade, and those who battled here are said to have received the same spiritual benefits as those who battled in the Holy Land. It was believed that if you fought in a Crusade, your sins were forgiven, and if you died, your soul would have a place in Heaven. At one point in time, the Pope forbade any knights from Spain to go and fight in the Holy Land. The Reconquest of Spain was what originally drew the Knights Templar to the region, and later, as the Moors were pushed back, their role changed to that of protectors and bankers for pilgrims.

Through the subsequent centuries, the Kingdom of Asturias fragmented into the kingdoms of Aragon, Navarra, Castilla,

NAVARRA
NAFARROA

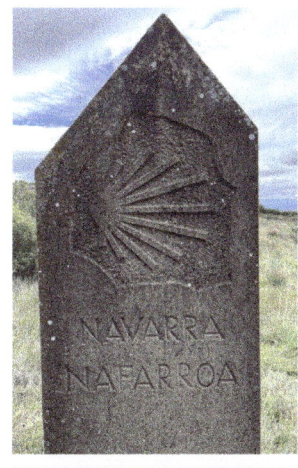

Leon, Galicia, and later Portugal, each playing its part in medieval geopolitics and the expansion of the Camino de Santiago.

After crossing the border, you have two choices. You can continue on to Sangüesa or take a detour to Javier. I recommend going to Javier, which has a medieval castle.

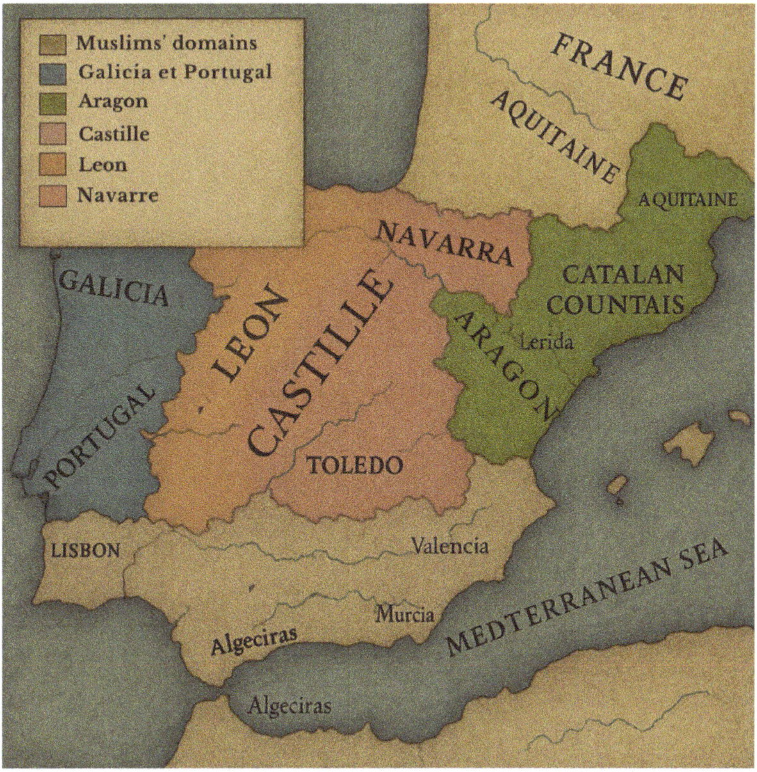
Muslims' domains
Galicia et Portugal
Aragon
Castille
Leon
Navarre
FRANCE
AQUITAINE
AQUITAINE
NAVARRA
CATALAN COUNTAIS
GALICIA
LEON
CASTILLE
ARAGON
Lerida
PORTUGAL
TOLEDO
LISBON
Valencia
MEDTERRANEAN SEA
Murcia
Algeciras
Algeciras

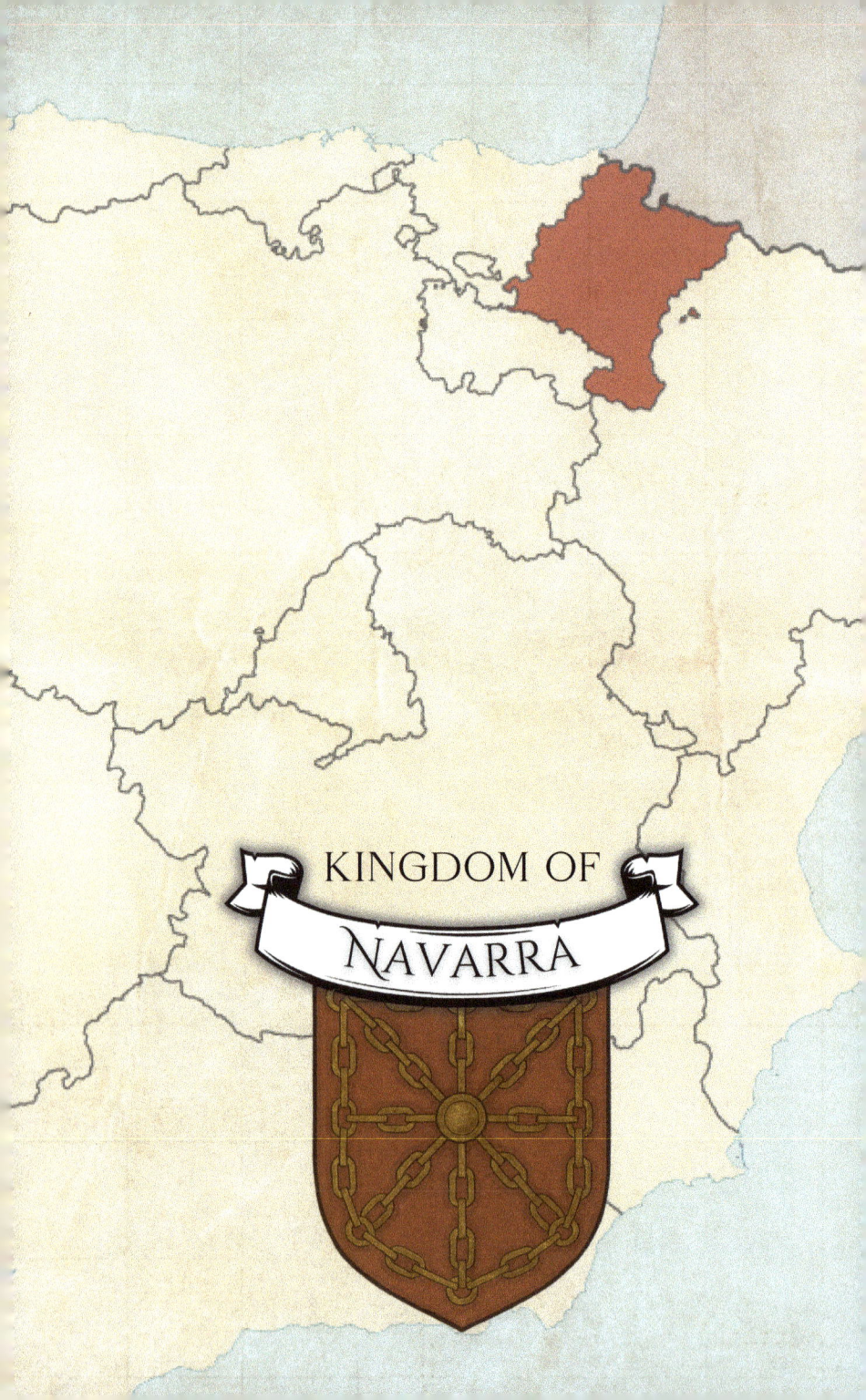

KINGDOM OF

NAVARRA

DAY 5:
SANGÜESA - MONREAL | 27.2 KM

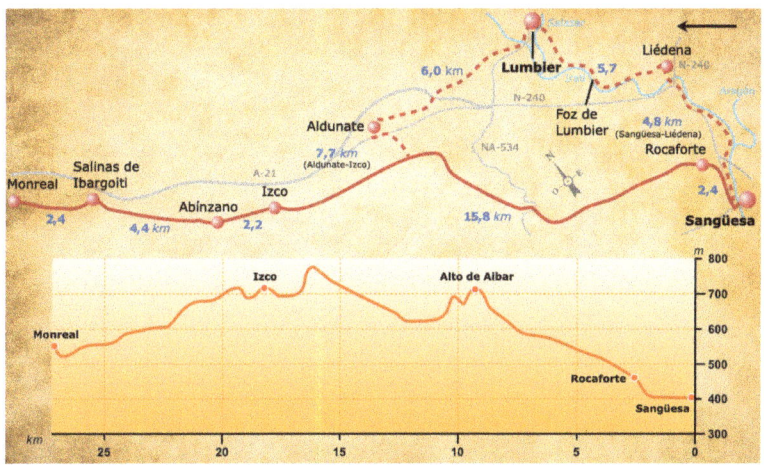

Sanguesa was founded in 1122 by Alfonso the Battler, King of Aragon and Navarre. He would also later become king of Leon, Castile, and Galicia through his marriage to Urraca. Alfonso the Battler is one of the main reasons why the Templars' Camino begins in Aragon. We have hinted at his importance before this chapter, but now it's time for a deep dive.

Alfonso the Battler lived from 1073 to 1134. In life, he was a great fighter and won several battles in the Reconquest of Spain. He had close associations with the Templars and was also known as the keeper of the Holy Grail. What is even more fascinating is that in death, he willed the entire kingdom to the Church of the Holy Sepulchre in the Holy Land, the

Knights Hospitaller—another military order formed in the Holy Land, and to the Templars. He also willed all of the horses in his cavalry to the Templars. The orders refused, but the Templars settled for many lands, as well as control over mills and graineries, which gave them control over the means of production in the land.

When he died, his body was secretly taken away instead of being laid to rest in San Juan de La Peña, as other monarchs had before him. The public didn't know he had died until his brother Ramiro, who was a Cluny monk, was taken out of the monastery and declared King.

The story becomes more interesting forty-four years later. In 1177, King Alfonso II, the grandnephew of Alfonso the Battler, began to redistribute castles and land that had belonged to the Templars. Almost immediately after this happened, rumors spread that Alfonso the Battler had returned from the dead. A man appeared, claiming to be him. Many Aragonese nobles and the members of the public believed that he was the king returned from the dead. The story concludes with the false king being hanged and then taken back to the same tomb where the Battler had supposedly been buried before.

Could this story give credence to the legend that Alfonso the Battler was actually the keeper of the Holy Grail—the chalice that was said to give eternal life?

Continuing the journey from Sangüesa, there is a 15 km stretch of pastureland with many free horses. Could some of these horses be the descendants of those that Alfonso willed to the Templars?

DAY 6:
MONREAL - PUENTE LA REINA | 31 KM

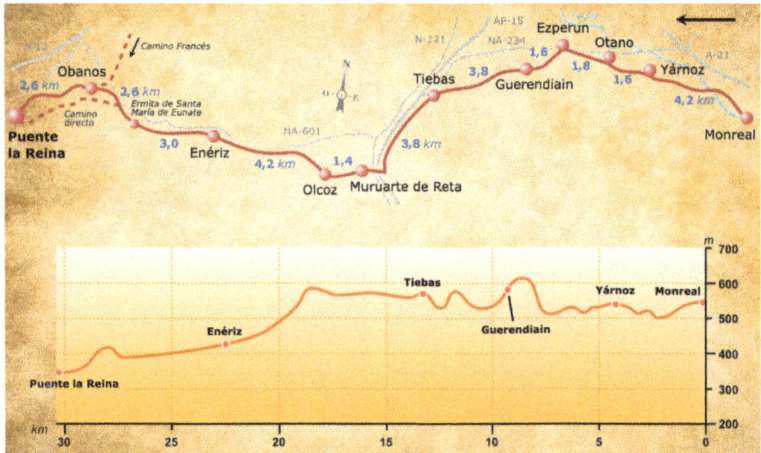

Today is your last day on the Aragonese Camino. This stretch takes us from Monreal to Puente la Reina, where we will meet up with the Camino Frances and two amazing Templar sites. Enjoy this last day of solitude and prepare yourself for a different kind of Camino.

Five kilometers before reaching Puente la Reina, you encounter the Church of Santa Maria de Eunate. This church is one of the best examples of an octagonal church on the Camino de Santiago. Although historical details about the church's origins remain elusive, the symbolism and design suggest a connection to the Templar order, especially since it is only five kilometers from the largest Templar commandery in the region.

The octagonal design of the Church of Eunate mirrors that of the Templars' iconic headquarters in Jerusalem – a structure known today as the Dome of the Rock. Originally, this structure was built as a mosque on the site where Solomon's Temple once stood. It is also said that Muhammad was taken from within this mosque to the heavens by the angel Gabriel and shown paradise.

During the Crusades, the Templars used this mosque as their headquarters in Jerusalem. They received the name Templars because they occupied the site of Solomon's Temple. You can see this octagonal design on the Templars' emblem. After the Crusades, the Templars' headquarters was converted back into a mosque once more.

 Upon arrival at Puente la Reina, you will pass through a giant gate to enter the walled city. During the medieval times, this gate would be closed if the plague was detected on the Camino de Santiago, halting the progression of pilgrims, as none could cross the river that lay on the other side of the city.

After you pass through the gate, to your right is the Iglesia del Crucifijo, and to your left is an entrance to what was once the largest Templar headquarters, also known as a commandery, in the region. Upon entering the Iglesia del Crucifijo, to the left of the altar, you will find a crucifix shaped like a goosefoot—a symbol intricately connected with the Templars.

The goose was seen as a wise animal, just as the Templars were considered wise. The goose is also white, just like the Templars' mantle. The goosefoot was also a symbol of the Agots, a people who were the builders for the Templars.

On the Camino de Santiago, it is also believed that the goosefoot is a symbol for the three main Camino paths, which converge near Puente la Reina. The Camino Aragonese is the path we have been following from the south. To the North is the Camino Baztanes, which connects in Pamplona. Coming straight across is the Camino Frances, the path we will now be following.

The goose symbol has another important meaning to both the Templars and the Camino, but this will be discussed in a few days when we reach Logroño.

29

DAY 7:
Puenta la Reina to Estella | 21.6 KM

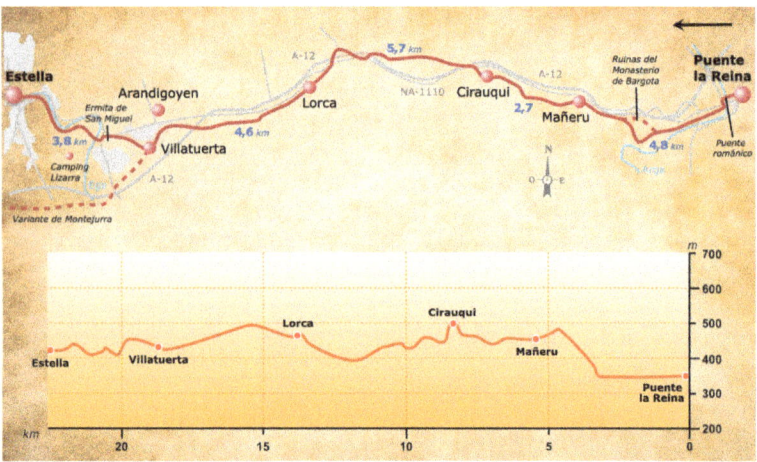

True adventure often starts before the sun rises. I encourage you to start your journey in the wee hours of the morning. There is a long stretch of the Camino, just outside of Puente la Reina, that is straight and flat, creating the perfect opportunity to walk under the stars. If the moon is full, you won't even need a flashlight!

Upon entering Estella, keep an eye out for a distinctive door near the town's entrance adorned with a Tau Cross. This simple yet powerful symbol holds deep significance, particularly in Templar lore. The Tau Cross, shaped like the Greek letter

"T," represents both the cross of crucifixion and the staff of the ancient Egyptian god Osiris. On the Templars' Camino, this symbol appears several times and is intertwined with a powerful family believed to have strong associations with the Templars.

In the heart of Estella, rising high above the city, is the Iglesia de San Miguel. Making the journey up the steep climb is well worth it. At the entrance to the church, you will find an intricately carved facade with some unexpected aspects. To the left of the door, you will see a carving of two alchemists at work, and to the right of the door, you will find the eight-pointed Alchemic Star. The eight-pointed star has many different meanings in many different religions and traditions. In alchemy, the eight-pointed star represents harmony and balance. It also represents the four elements (fire, water, earth, and air) and the four qualities (hot, cold, wet, and dry) that were believed to make up all matter.

Alchemy—an ancient practice blending science, philosophy, and spirituality—holds a curious connection to the Templars. It is believed that Templar knights, while engaged in their military and spiritual duties, also delved into the esoteric realms of alchemical knowledge. The carving serves as a tangible reminder of the Templars' quest for hidden truths and spiritual transformation. Some also believe that the treasure the Templars found under Solomon's Temple was these alchemical secrets.

DAY 8:
ESTELLA - LOS ARCOS | 21.3 KM

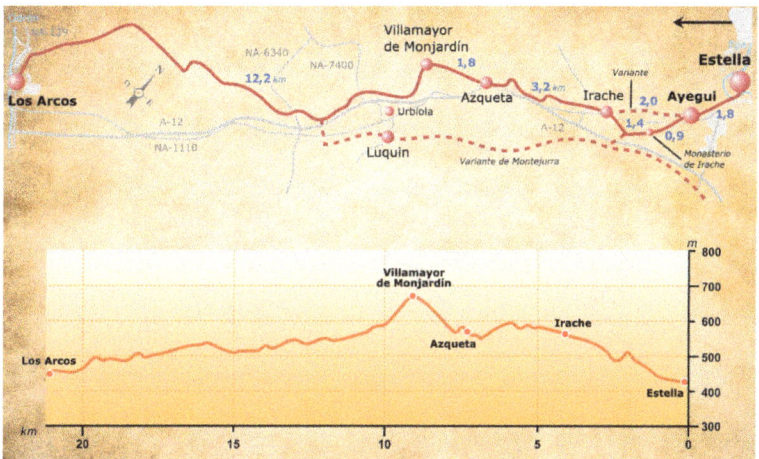

Just outside of Estella, you will come across a blacksmith. I highly recommend taking a few moments to watch him work at his forge. His work is filled with Templar symbolism that we have discussed so far. My favorite pieces are his Camino shells with either the Templar Cross, Goosefoot, Tau, or Cross of St. James (not a Templar symbol). Over 700 years after the Templars were disbanded, their symbols still persist on the Camino today. It is fun to lose yourself at the blacksmith's shop and imagine him forging a sword for your quest!

Past the blacksmith, there is a fountain where you can get either water or wine. It is one of the most famous spots on the Camino. Take a moment to have a refreshment before you continue. Shortly after this, the Camino splits into two. I recommend taking the alternate route to the left, which will take you into the mountains with breathtaking views of the fields below.

Arriving in Los Arcos, take a moment to explore the Church of Santa Maria Los Arcos. Inside is one of the most beautiful cloistered gardens on the Camino. One can imagine a medicinal garden of the Templars here, with monks tending to the plants as they live the contemplative lives.

DAY 9:
LOS ARCOS - LOGROÑO | 27.6 KM

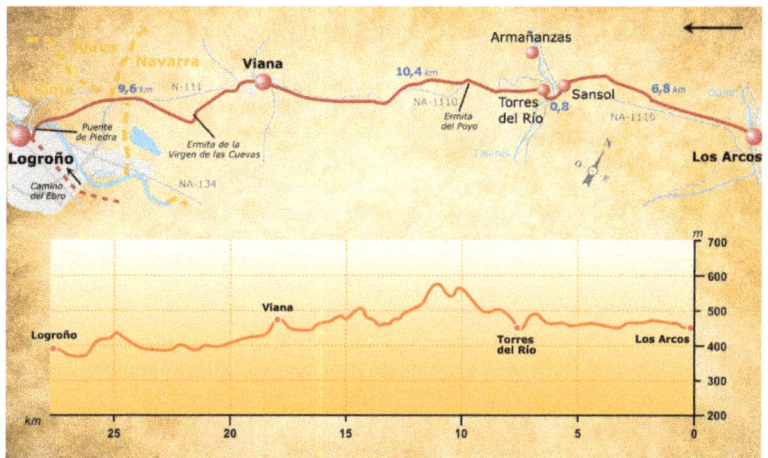

About 6.8 km outside of Los Arcos is Sansol. Take a moment to step off the Camino and visit the Iglesia de San Zoilo. Here, you will find a Templar Cross on the pavement in front of the church. Also, from here, you can see the Iglesia del San Sepulcro in Torres del Río 0.8 km away. The two churches bring to mind the church of the Holy Sepulchre in Jerusalem and the Templars' headquarters on the site where Solomon's Temple once stood.

The Iglesia del San Sepulcro is another eight-sided church, leading us to believe it is of Templar construction. On the central dome of the church, you will once again find the Alchemist Star constructed from the church's crossbeams. Another interesting observation is that the domes of the church, when combined, create the number eight.

The adventure along the Camino de Santiago leads you to the vibrant city of Logroño, situated approximately 20 km (12.43 miles) from Torres del Río. Here, amidst the bustling streets and historic landmarks, lies a secret that we have been hinting at in previous chapters.

In Logroño, seek out the giant board game called "The Game of the Goose," next to the Church of Santiago el Real. This game is said to have been created by the Knights Templar as a way to pass the time, but it also holds another meaning. This ancient game, dating back to the Middle Ages, holds symbolic significance for pilgrims on the Camino de Santiago. The journey of the goose, depicted on the board, mirrors the Camino de Santiago itself. Several squares on the board line up with geographical locations on the Camino, and there are geese (a symbol of the Templars) located in squares that line up with known Templar sites.

Could this board game be an encoded Templar map of the Camino de Santiago? If so, what does it hide?

As you navigate through the game, pay attention to spaces six and twelve, representing the bridges of Puente la Reina and Logroño, respectively. These bridges, integral to medieval trade routes, may have played a role in the Templars' commerce and logistics along the Camino. Hypothesize about the Templars' strategic use of these waterways to transport goods and maintain their network of commanderies and resources.

After exploring the Templar symbolism embedded in "The Game of the Goose," take time to savor the culinary delights of Logroño. Indulge in the local tradition of pinchos, sampling an array of savory bites and regional specialties all served on small plates. The communal atmosphere of sharing small plates with fellow pilgrims and locals alike fosters a sense of camaraderie and celebration, making for a memorable experience in this lively city.

DAY 10:
LOGROÑO - NÁJERA | 29 KM

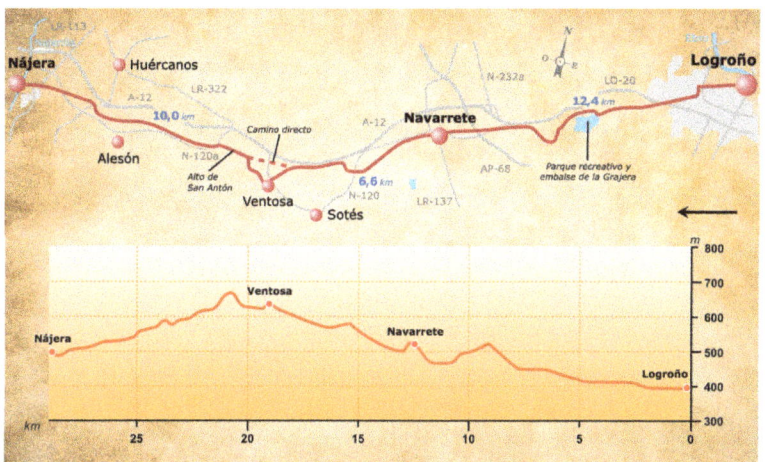

Before you reach the town of Navarrete, after the steep descent, you might encounter a man in his fifties who will ask you if he can walk with you to practice his English. If you get the opportunity, say yes. I have had the pleasure of walking with him twice and have learned much about the history of the Templars on the Camino de Santiago, as well as the history of the Reconquest of Spain.

About six hours after leaving Logroño, you will arrive in Nájera. Make sure that you pass from the modern city to the old city on the other side of the bridge. There is a lovely Albergue

Municipal there. After you cross the bridge, you will encounter the image and poem featured at the beginning of this book. It is another echo of the Templars' past and presence in this area. Nájera is famous for the legend of the cave, which contained an image of the Virgin Mary. According to this legend, King Don Garcia Sanchez III discovered this image while hunting with his falcon in 1052. After this discovery, the cave became the burial place for the Kings and the members of the royal family of Pamplona-Najera. Today, the cave is encapsulated by the Monastery of Santa Maria la Real. Could this mysterious image have been made by the Templars?

The Templars held the Virgin Mary and the sacred feminine in the highest esteem. It is also believed that they were responsible for propagating the Cult of the Virgin Mary. This worship of the Virgin Mary spread across Europe in the Middle Ages and is still present today. But, could the worship of the Virgin Mary have held a dual purpose?

Oftentimes, Christianity has adopted pagan rituals and incorporated them into Christian practice to ease the transition from paganism to Christianity. An example of this is the Christmas tree, which traces back to the tradition of Yuletide. During Yuletide, pagans would bring fir trees into their homes and decorate them with candles. Here, we might see another example of this with the Basque worship of Mari.

Mari was the main goddess of ancient Basque mythology. She was a nature deity who was said to live on Mount Anboto. The etymology of the name Mari is related to the word Amari, which means "mother." It wouldn't be a far stretch to go from worshiping Mother Mari to Mother Mary.

DAY 11:
Nájera to Santo Domingo de Calzada | 20.7 km

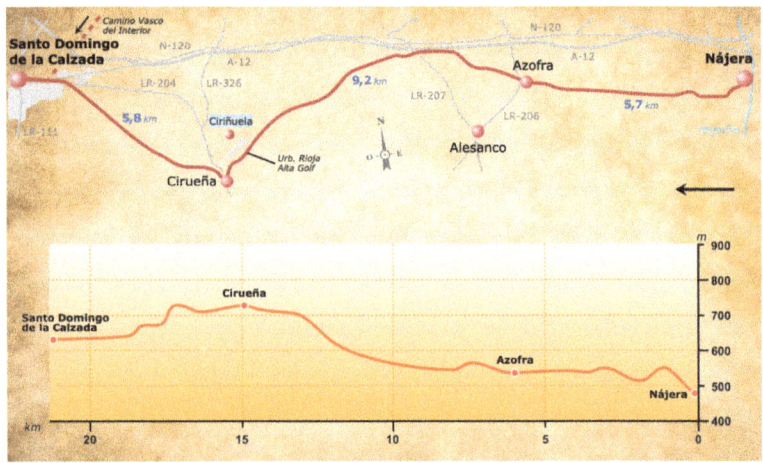

Leaving Nájera, there is a slight uphill, then a straight shot to Azofra. I would recommend getting a snack and something to drink here, as it is just over nine kilometers to the next town. I would also recommend using the restroom, as the walk is fairly exposed, with open fields on each side.

Fifteen kilometers from Azofra is Santo Domingo de la Calzada. This historic town doesn't have any direct connection with the Templars, but it is steeped in legend and lore. The town takes its name from Saint Domingo García, a revered figure whose life and works shaped the landscape of pilgrimage in medieval Spain. Born in Viloria de la Rioja in 1019, Domingo

García, later known as Santo Domingo de la Calzada, embarked on a journey of faith and service. He dedicated himself to aiding pilgrims along the Camino de Santiago. His efforts included constructing bridges, hospices, and roads, earning him the nickname "De la Calzada."

The cathedral of Santo Domingo de la Calzada boasts a unique feature - a chicken coop housing a white rooster and hen. Legend has it that these birds serve as a reminder of a miraculous event associated with the town. A German pilgrim accused of theft was unjustly hanged, for a crime he didn't commit. Knowing there was nothing they could do for their son, the family continued on to Santiago de Compostela. On their return, the pilgrim's family found their son still hanging at the crossroads, but he was alive.

They ran to the magistrate, who was having dinner. The family told him that their son was still alive, and the judge said he was as alive as the chicken on his plate. At that moment, the chicken sprang to life, confirming the innocence of the accused. This miraculous event is immortalized in the Codex Calixtinus, which was essentially the first guidebook ever created. It contains accounts of miracles attributed to Saint James and practical advice for travelers on the Camino.

KINGDOM OF

CASTILLA

DAY 12:
SANTO DOMINGO DE LA CALZADA TO BELORADO | 21.8 KM

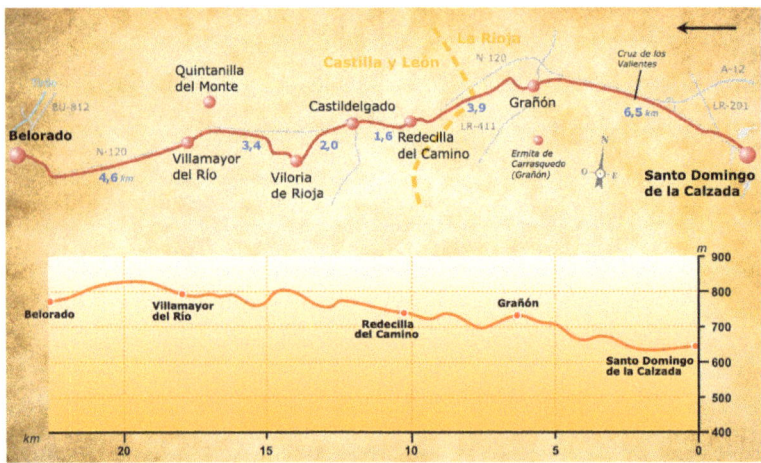

B elorado's origins trace back to ancient times, with Celti-berian and Roman settlements dotting its landscape. The town's strategic location between the Meseta and the Ebro Valley made it a vital crossroads for trade and pilgrimage. As pilgrims traversed the Camino de Santiago, Belorado provided a place of rest and refuge before the perilous journey through the Montes de Oca forests. (Mountain of Geese)

During the medieval period, Belorado played a pivotal role in the border disputes between the kingdoms of Navarre and

Castile. The town's fortress, originally constructed to defend against invasion, became a symbol of power and control in the region. It is said to have been this way until Alfonso the Battler of Aragon brought peace to the region.

Under Alfonso the Battler, Belorado flourished as a mercantile center. Its position on the north face of the Sierra de la Demanda attracted merchants and traders from afar. Despite political upheavals in later centuries, Belorado's mercantile spirit endured, shaping its cultural and economic landscape.

Dive deeper into Belorado's history by visiting its medieval castle ruins, perched atop a mount overlooking the town and venture beyond the town limits to discover the Puras Mining Complex (this will be mentioned later in reference to the Templars) and the caves of Fuentemolinos. Guided tours of the mining complex offer insights into the region's mining heritage, while visits to the caves reveal underground rivers and unique rock formations.

DAY 13:

BELORADO TO SAN JUAN DE ORTEGA | 23.9 KM

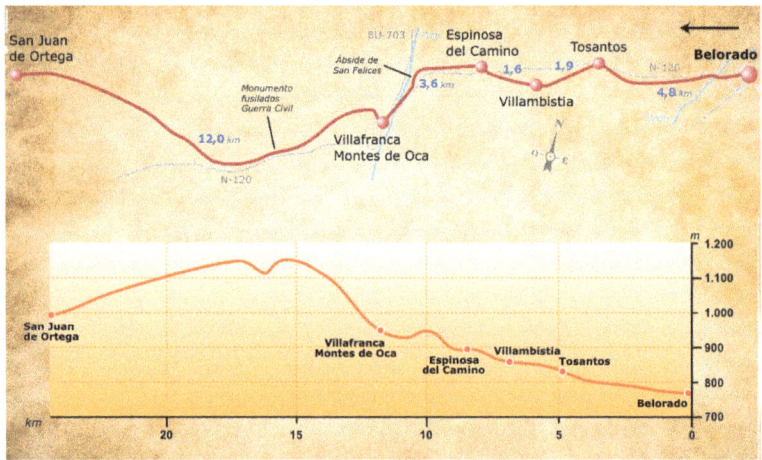

On the way to San Juan de Ortega, we pass through Villafranca Montes de Oca. Here we find the Rio Oca as well as the Montes de Oca. As established before, the Templars were associated with the word Oca (Goose) because the Goose was seen as a wise animal, just as the Templars were considered wise. The Templars also wore white, just like the feathers of a goose. On this section of the Camino, we find another connection to the Templars and the Game of the Goose—Juego de la Oca.

In the Game of the Goose, there are thirteen squares that contain a goose symbol. The first appears at Eunate, where we visited the Templars' octagonal church. The second is at Torres del Rio, where we visited the Templars' second octagonal church—Iglesia del Santo Sepulcro. The third goose appears at Nájera, where we find the veneration of the Virgin Mary. The fourth appears at Villafranca de los Montes de Oca. Translated, montes means mountains, and Oca is goose. Here, once again, we see the relationship between the Templars, the Camino de Santiago, and the Game of the Goose.

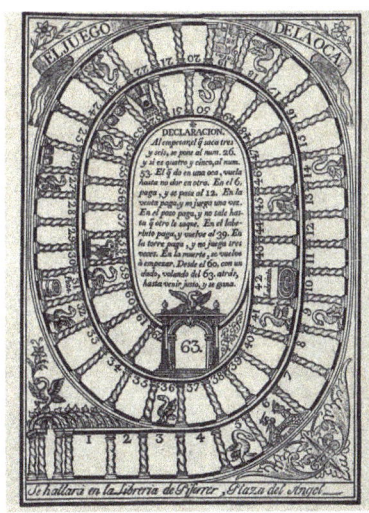 

The Templars held a profound reverence for sacred sites and hidden knowledge. It is believed that these goose squares held a special importance to them, serving as markers of spiritual significance and repositories of ancient wisdom. But could the geese in the game have also been a sign of their treasure as well?

The Templars became an incredibly wealthy organization through land donations and acting as bankers for pilgrims as well as for the monarchy. But, it is also believed that they found great treasures under Solomon's Temple during their occupation of Jerusalem, both physical and spiritual. It is also rumored that the treasure disappeared along with a majority of the Templars on Friday, October 13th, 1307. Could these Goose Squares hold the clues to where it is.

Close to Villafranca Montes de Oca lie remnants of two Roman forts—La Pedraja and Somorrostro, which, combined with the nearby Puras Mining Complex, add another layer to the puzzle. Could it be that the Romans once mined these lands for precious resources, laying the groundwork for future exploitation by the Templars?

DAY 14:
SAN JUAN DE ORTEGA TO BURGOS | 25.8 KM

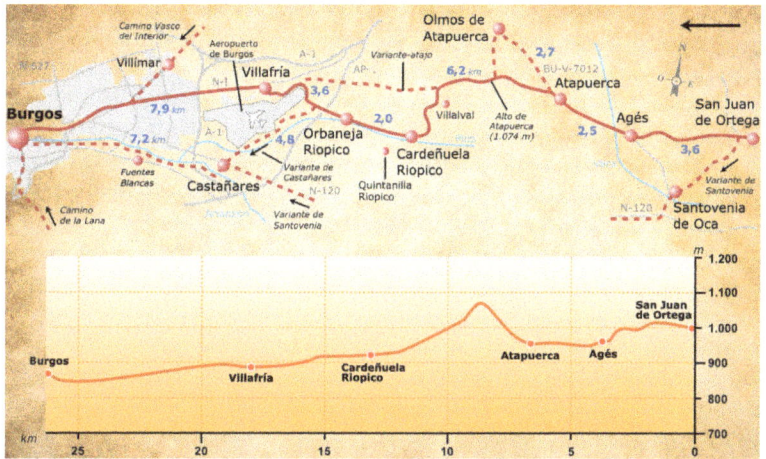

S an Juan de Ortega owes its name to the revered saint, Juan de Ortega, whose miraculous birth and divine deeds are steeped in legend and lore. Born in Quintanaortuño in 1088, Juan's towering stature, both physical and spiritual, earned him a place among the giants of medieval history. The sanctuary of San Juan de Ortega, with its captivating architecture and sacred relics, bears witness to the enduring legacy of this holy figure.

There isn't any direct connection to the Templars here, but it is worth mentioning the Miracle of Light. At five o'clock in the evening on the equinox, inside the chapel where San Juan is buried, there has been observed what has become known as the Miracle of Light. Precisely on these days and times, a shaft of light shines in and rests on a sculpture of the Archangel Gabriel announcing to Mary that she will have a child. This is

important as the sanctuary has long been associated with fertility.

On the way to Burgos, we also pass through Atapuerca. Just before you reach the city, you will pass the caves of the Sierra de Atapuerca. The entrance to the road is marked by a sign and a megalithic stone structure. These caves are considered one of Europe's most important paleontological sites. Inside is a fossil record of Europe's oldest human beings, dating back to almost a million years ago. If you have time, it is definitely worth the stop.

฿URGOS:

Continuing on to Burgos, the Camino splits. I recommend taking the alternative route that passes by the airport and leads you into the city via the river. This entrance is one of the most spectacular on the Camino. You walk through the ornately decorated gate in the city wall and enter a giant courtyard with the cathedral waiting for you.

Founded in the ninth century, Burgos flourished as a center of culture, commerce, and spirituality. Among the Templars' areas of interest were Kabbalah and sacred geometry, ancient systems of knowledge that held the keys to unlocking the mysteries of the universe.

The history of Kabbalah in Burgos is deeply intertwined with the city's rich cultural and religious heritage. Kabbalah, a mystical tradition within Judaism, has roots dating back to ancient times, but it flourished particularly during the Middle Ages, finding fertile ground among Jewish communities in Spain, including Burgos.

During the medieval period, Burgos was a vibrant center of Jewish life and scholarship. The Jewish quarter, known as the Judería, thrived as a hub of intellectual and spiritual exchange, where scholars from across Europe converged to study and debate philosophical and mystical ideas.

Kabbalah, with its esoteric teachings and mystical interpretations of Jewish scripture, captivated the minds of scholars and seekers in Burgos. Influenced by both Jewish mysticism and the broader currents of medieval European thought, Kabbalistic ideas took root and flourished within the city's Jewish community.

One of the most significant figures in the history of Kabbalah in Burgos was Rabbi Moses de León, a renowned Kabbalist who lived in the thirteenth century. De León is credited with authoring the Zohar, one of the foundational texts of Kabbalah. The Zohar, written in Aramaic, expounds upon the mystical teachings of the Torah and explores the nature of God, the universe, and the soul.

De León's teachings and the spread of Kabbalistic ideas in Burgos had a profound influence on Jewish spirituality and mysticism throughout Spain and beyond. The city became a beacon of Kabbalistic learning, attracting scholars and practitioners from far and wide.

DAY 15:
BURGOS TO THE ARC
OF SAN ANTON | 39 KM

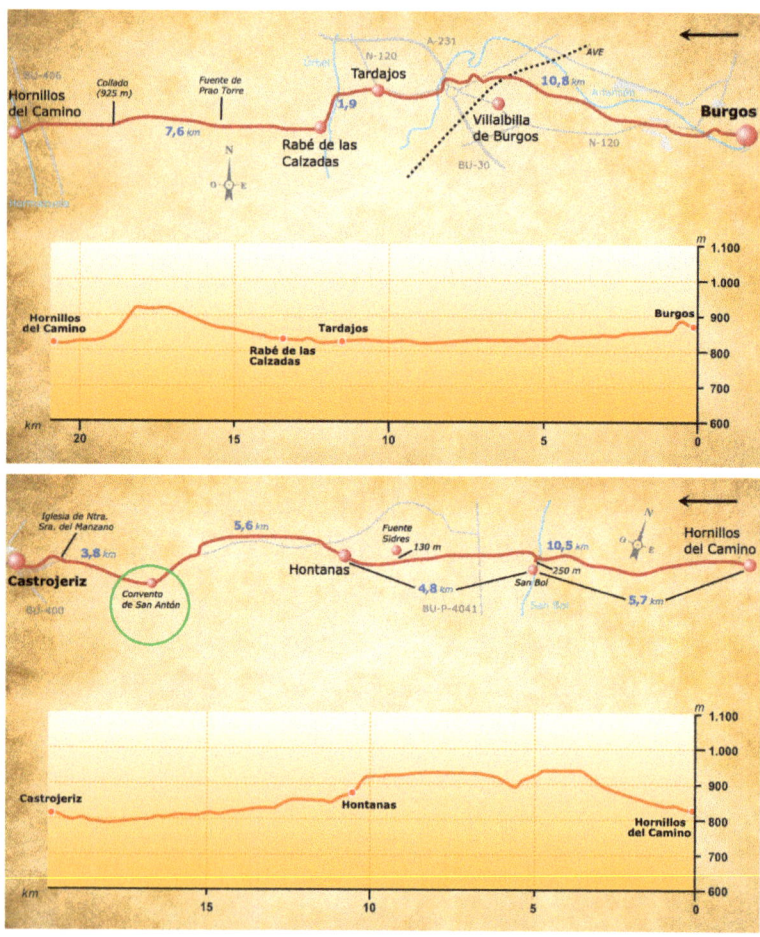

ontinuing our journey from Burgos, you have two choices. The first is to stop at Hornillos del Camino, 20.3 km or to continue on to the Arc of San Anton, nearly 39 km (24.34 miles).

I recommend pushing through, if you can, to the Arc of San Anton. This is one of my favorite places on the Camino and is not to be missed. Here, you can sleep in the ruins of one of the most moving structures on the Camino de Santiago. Space is limited, so try to arrive as early as you can.

The Arc of San Anton was said to have belonged to the San Antonian monks. This became a famous destination in the Middle Ages as pilgrims would travel thousands of miles to come here to be treated for the Fire of San Anton—a disease that mimicked the plague and often induced hallucinations.

Those who braved making the journey were miraculously cured of the disease at the Arc but suffered the affliction when they returned home. It was later discovered that the Fire of San Anton was caused by a fungus that grew on grain. This fungus couldn't survive in the arid landscape around the Arc.

One of the most prominent features of the Arc of San Anton is the Tau window. The Tau was a sign of protection and was conferred upon the Antonian monks. However, the Tau can also mean T.H. or Templum Hierosolyma, Temple of Jerusalem, a reference to King Solomon's Temple, the destroyed repository of ancient artifacts, including the Ark of the Covenant. And in translation (Theca ubi res pretiosa), the sign has a double meaning as "a key to the treasure" and/or "a place where the precious things are concealed." Could the Ark of the Covenant once been stored here?

The Tau symbol is also associated with the Lemón family who originated in this region and continues to show up in relation to the Knights Templar again and again on the Camino. One other interesting fact to remember about the Lemón family is that the symbol of their family crest is a six-sided dice. We will talk more about that later.

The Arc of San Anton and Castrojeriz (3.9k away) align with space 23 on the Game of the Goose. This space contains the next goose square on the playing board. Here, once again, we find a treasure trove of the Templars' legacy.

The Arc of San Anton serves as a reminder of the journey's healing properties and hidden treasures. As you stay the night in this ancient ruin, gaze upon the stars in the courtyard and be transported back to a time when the Templars roamed this land.

At the Arc of San Anton, you are awakened by soft candlelight from the kitchen, as the Arc has no electricity. Enjoy your candlelit breakfast at the Arc of San Anton before setting out on your journey. Instead of traveling on the main road the 3.9 km to Castrojeriz, exit through the side entrance and venture to the Convento de Santa Clara for morning mass.

For over 500 years, twenty-four hours a day, a nun has been in observance of the Holy Eucharist at Santa Clara. The nuns here live a cloistered life, but you can speak briefly with one of them from behind a wall if you buy some of their home-made cookies.

From here, continue on to Castrojeriz. This small town holds a special place in my heart. When I first visited Castrojeriz in 2016, it was the first time I was told about the Knights Templar on the Camino de Santiago. In a late-night conversation with a hospitalero, I was told that there were five former Templar commanderies associated with Castrojeriz and the surrounding area. The Arc of San Anton and the Convent of Santa Clara were numbered amongst these five. I was told that after the Templars were disbanded, they either switched the order they belonged to, as in becoming Antonians, or transferred owner-ship of the property.

IGLESIA DE SANTA MARIA DEL MANZANO: POSSIBLE FORMER TEMPLAR COMMANDERY

At the entrance to Castrojeriz from the traditional Camino path is the church of Santa Maria del Manzano. Do not pass this gem by. Once again, in the northeast section of the church, is a very interesting sight. Here lies a sarcophagus with the effigy of two knights carved on top. This is reminiscent of the Templar seal of two knights riding one horse.

On the coffin, there are two right hands with pentagrams on them. This symbol is known as the Seal of Solomon. It is said that this symbol was on Solomon's ring and gave him power over evil spirits. This symbol takes us back to Solomon's Temple, where the Templars were first founded. The pentagram is also associated with alchemy, representing the five elements, Kabbalah, and Christianity, and representing the five wounds of Jesus. To the top left of each hand, we also find a Seed of Life.

IGLESIA DE SANTO DOMINGO: POSSIBLE FORMER TEMPLAR COMMANDERY

The second church we come to in town is the Iglesia de Santo Domingo. This church has been converted into a museum so some of its originality has been lost, but as you pass, take a minute to observe the two skulls and crossbones with the inscriptions "O mors," and "O aeternitas," which translate to, "Oh death," and "Oh eternity." Take a moment to reflect on your own mortality as you pass.

IGLESIA DE SAN JUAN: POSSIBLE FORMER TEMPLAR COMMANDERY

Signs of the Templars are etched into the very stone of this church. On the pillars, you will find a carving of a Templar Cross as well as masons' marks, which were used to denote which quarry a stone came from. On the back of the church is a pentagram stained-glass window.

We have already discussed some meanings for the pentagram, but one other meaning is a symbol for Venus, as the celestial body traces a pentagram path across the sky every eight years. Take a moment to venture into the courtyard. Here, carved into the covered walkway, you will see several Kabbalistic images, including the Seed of Life and the Flower of Life, once again tying the Templars in with Kabbalah.

One other interesting fact about Castrojeriz is that there are tunnels that lead from the city all the way up the hill to the castle. Were these dug by the Templars, who were known for their expertise in excavation?

Enjoy a full rest day wandering the chapels of Castrojeriz in search of ancient symbols and hidden wisdom.

DAY 17:
CASTROJERIZ TO FROMISTA | 24.7 KM

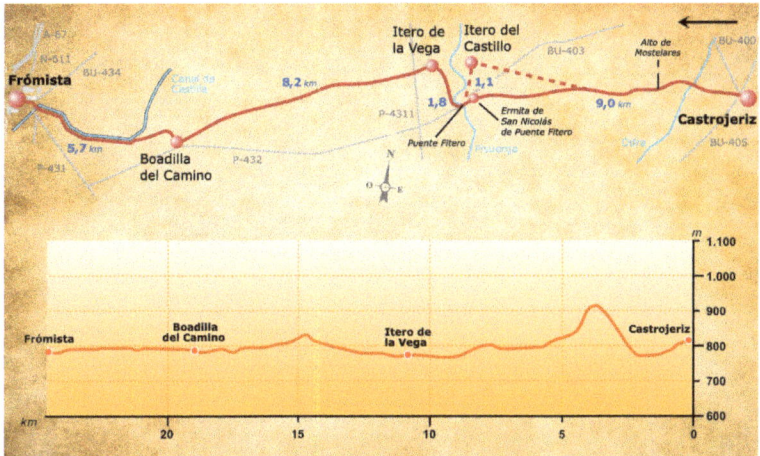

After the day of rest in Castrojeriz, you will be energized to do the 24 km (15 miles) walk to Frómist, but I recommend stopping in Boadilla del Camino. This little town doesn't have much, but it has an amazing Albergue run by kind people. The Albergue En El Camino has a cloistered garden and pool where you can swim or soak your feet. The other reason I have you stopping here is that tomorrow there is going to be a lot to see, and if you start too early, the churches will be closed.

If you choose to carry on to Frómista, you will find our next Templar site, the church of San Martín de Frómista. Founded in 1066 as a monastery, this church also has an octagonal dome that tops the transept. As we have learned in previous chapters, this style of church is associated with the Templars. Also, in regard to the Game of the Goose, the next Goose square falls here or at Villalcazar de Sirga, which we will explore tomorrow.

DAY 18:
FORMISTA TO CARRIÓN DE LOS CONDES | 18.8 KM

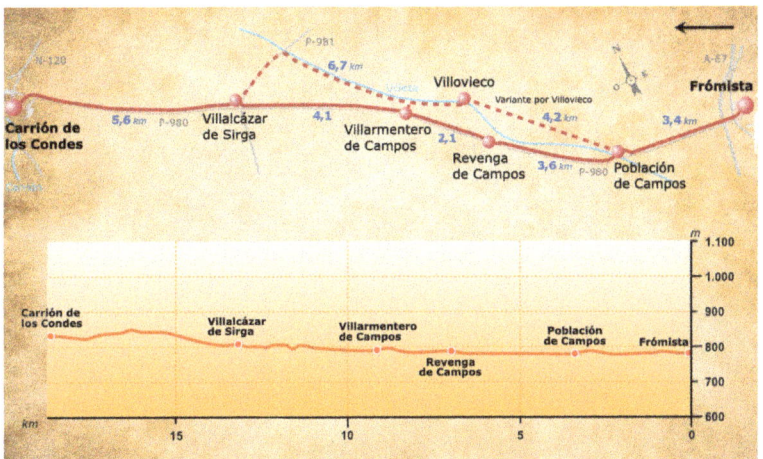

Enjoy a lie-in as the churches we are going to visit today don't open until 9:00 am. From Frómista, you will continue on to the next place of Templar interest, Villalcázar de Sirga.

Villalcázar de Sirga is rumored to have been the town where the Templar Commandery of Villalcazar was located. Evidence of this can be seen inside the Iglesia de Santa Maria la Blanca. The church has many symbols and legends pointing to the Templars, including several images of Baphomet.

Baphomet, represented as a severed head, or in later years as a goat's head on a man's body, was the deity the Templars were accused of worshiping when they were put on trial. Inside this chapel and many others on the Camino, you will find images of the severed head. One theory on the origin of Baphomet is that if you put the Hebrew spelling into a Coptic cipher, it spells Sophia, which in Greek means wisdom. Could it have been that the Templars worshipped wisdom?

There is a legend that proposes on the equinox, a great Templar treasure will be revealed in this church. The legend says that on the equinox, a ray of light will hit the bull of the Pantocrator, and the mouth of the twelve heads will speak of where it is located.

Arriving at Carrión de Los Condes, make sure that you visit the Iglesia de Santa Maria del Camino. Here, you will find a goose-foot crucifix, another sure sign of the Templars' presence. I think that it is interesting that both here and in Hospital de Órbigo, you have a Goose Foot Crucifix and an Octagonal church less than a day's walk apart.

In the evening, I recommend that you stay with the singing nuns at the Albergue Parroquial Santa Maria del Camino. Here, both the nuns and the accommodations are nice. They have a great tradition of singing with the pilgrims, having pilgrims share something from their home country, and a communal dinner.

DAY 19:

CARRIÓN DE LOS CONDES TO TERRADILLOS DE LOS TEMPLARIOS | 26.3 KM

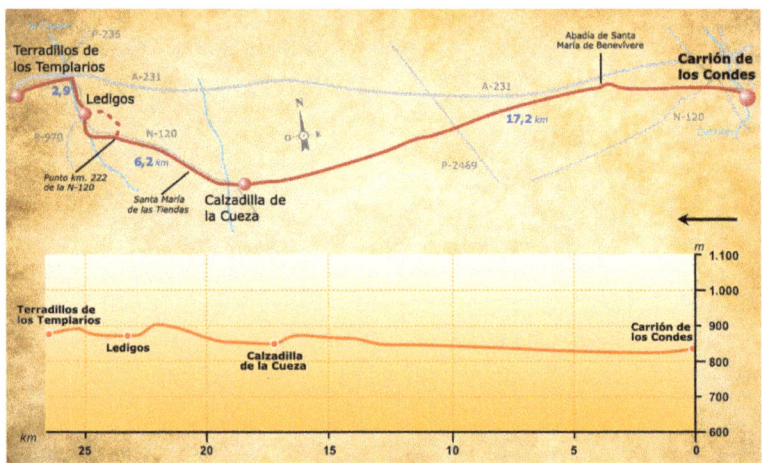

Leaving Carrión de los Condes, the Camino leads through the Spanish countryside, passing small villages and agricultural fields. As pilgrims approach Terradillos de Templarios, golden grain fields signal the region's rich farming tradition.

Terradillos de Templarios has a history tied to the Knights Templar. In 1191, King Alfonso VII of Castile is said to have donated the village to the Templars, who established an outpost to support their agricultural and logistical needs. The fertile lands likely helped sustain the order's operations both locally and abroad. There was also once a pilgrims' hospital nearby named San Juan.

A local legend claims Terradillos as the origin of the tale of the Goose that laid the golden egg. According to the story, the egg was brought to Santiago, but the priest there requested the goose itself. In response to this, the Templars buried the goose on a hill close to Terradillos de Templarios. This myth is often linked to the Templars' hidden wealth. The analogy also ties to King Philip IV of France, who sought the Templars' riches, only to find that their true strength lay in their organizational and productive capabilities.

The connection to the Templars extends to nearby Moratinos, home to another "goose square" in the Game of the Goose, the board game believed to reference Templar sites. This suggests a once-expansive Templar agricultural network in the area.

I recommend that you stay at the Albergue Jacques de Molay. This hostel is named after the last Grand Master of the Knights Templar. Once again, here we can see the connection between the Templars and this small town.

KINGDOM OF

LEON

DAY 20:
Terradillos de los Templarios to Mansilla de las Mulas |
53 KM

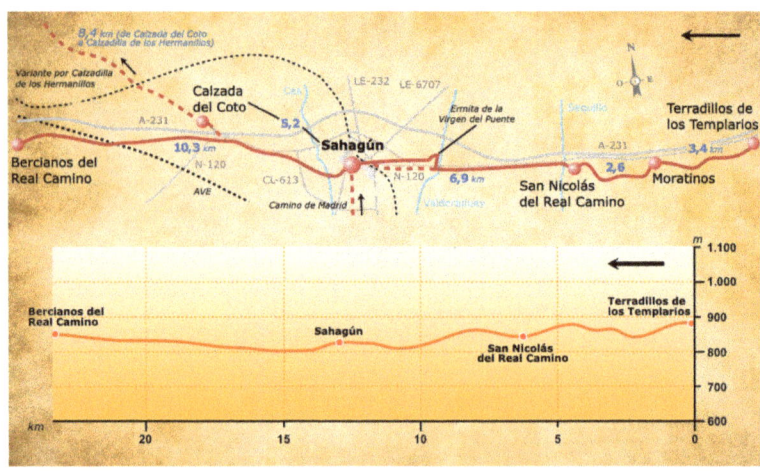

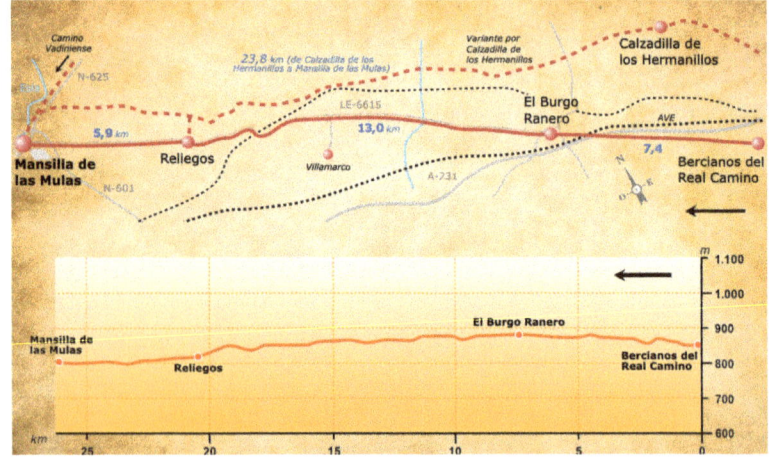

For this section, we will be traveling two stages of the Camino to Mansilla. The distance to Villamoros de Mansilla is approximately 53 km (32 miles) from Terradillos de Templarios. I recommend stopping at Bercianos del Real Camino (23 km) on the way for the evening.

Once a prominent Roman city, Villamoros de Mansilla played a key role in connecting ancient trade routes with the spiritual journeys of medieval pilgrims. Today, it reflects the rich history that defines the Camino de Santiago.

Near this ancient town lies a mysterious cave complex, rumored to have been the retreat of a solitary monk for centuries. This monk, according to local lore, maintained the spiritual sanctity of the place, drawing pilgrims and seekers of divine wisdom. Could this cave complex relate to the next goose square in the Game of the Goose?

DAY 21:
MANSILLA DE LAS MULAS
TO LEÓN | 18.5 KM

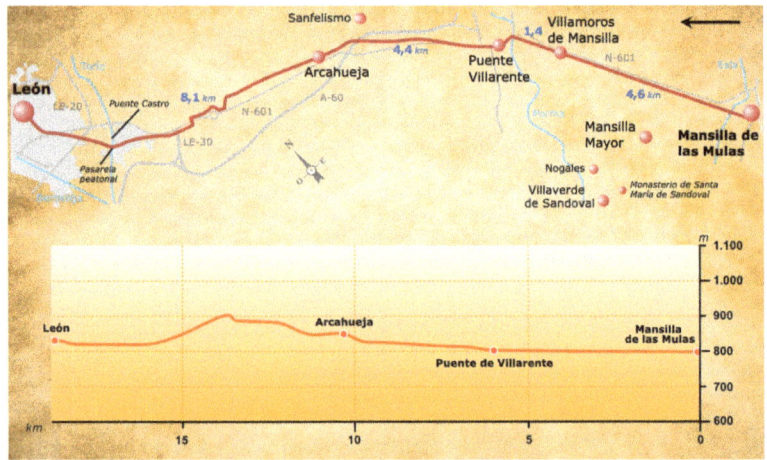

The journey to León spans approximately 18.5 kilometers from Mansilla de las Mulas, bringing pilgrims into one of the most significant historical and architectural cities along the Camino de Santiago.

León, a city rich with historical depth and architectural splendor, is home to the stunning León Cathedral, renowned for its impressive collection of stained-glass windows. The city's foundation stretches back to Roman times, evolving through the Visigothic era and flourishing as a kingdom in the Middle Ages. León became a vital center during the Reconquista, serving as a backdrop for the interplay of power among Christian kings.

While there is no direct evidence, there is speculation that the Templars helped to fund the construction of the Cathedral of León. If so, what message were they trying to leave behind in architecture for future generations to figure out? One of the most interesting highlights of the cathedral is the presence of "Green Men"—mysterious stone carvings depicting faces surrounded by or sprouting fol-lage from the mouth. These figures, which appear in various medieval European churches, including Rosslyn Chapel, are believed to symbolize rebirth and the intertwining of nature and humanity. Their presence in León Cathedral adds an intriguing pagan contrast to the predominantly Christian iconography.

Also, in the alcove chapel in the northeast corner of the cathedral that houses the original statue of the Virgin Blanco, there is a representation of Baphomet—a symbol connected with the Templars. If they did fund the cathedral, where did they get the money? This question will be answered in a later chapter.

In León, we find another Grail story as well. Inside the Museo San Isidoro de León is said to be the one true Holy Grail. The chalice is made of onyx and encrusted with gold and jewels. In Jesus' time, the cup would have only been made of stone, and the decorations were later added.

Legend has it that when the Taifa of Dénia, a medieval Islamic Kingdom in Spain that ruled over parts of the Valencian coast and Ibiza, was attacked by another Islamic kingdom, King Alfonso VI of Castilla and León came to its rescue. The king didn't see Dénia as a threat, and they worked in tandem. This indebted Dénia to the king.

Between 1064 and 1071, there was a famine in Egypt, and Egypt called on all of the Islamic kingdoms to send relief. Dénia was the only one who responded. Indebted to the small kingdom, Egypt asked Dénia what they wanted. In turn, Dénia asked King Alfonso what he wanted. His answer—the Holy Grail. With this, Egypt went to Jerusalem, which was under Muslim rule, and retrieved the Grail.

On the voyage from Spain, a great storm arose, and being afraid, one of the guards chipped off a piece of the Grail so he could keep it close to himself for protection. When the others found out, they seized the piece and threw him overboard. The Grial was delivered safely to Alfonso, but the chip was taken back to Egypt and can still be found today in a museum in Cairo.

King Alfonso VI later entrusted the Grail to his daughter Urraca, who is considered the first European queen to rule in her own right. Later, Urraca married Alfonso the Battler, whose story also ties in with the Grail legend, as we have spoken about earlier in our adventure.

DAY 22:
LEÓN TO HOSPITAL DE ÓRBIGO | 31.44 KM

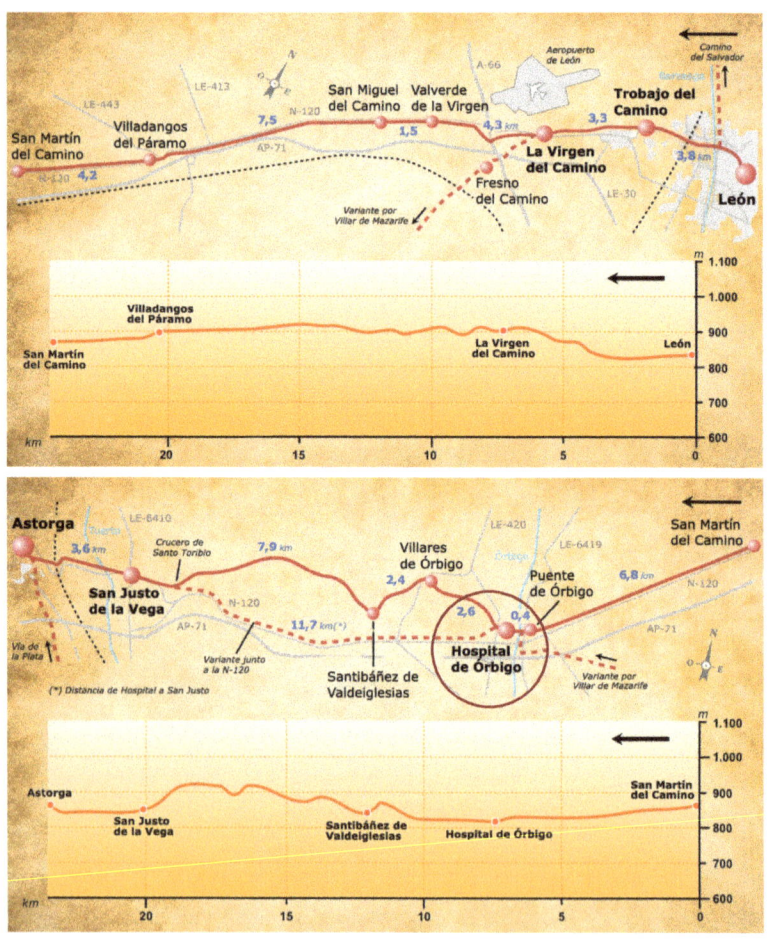

Hospital de Órbigo is renowned for its spectacular medieval bridge, the Puente de Órbigo, which stretches across the river, boasting nineteen arches. This bridge is not only a feat of medieval engineering but also the site of the legendary "passage of arms," an event where knight Don Suero de Quiñones once challenged passersby to a jousting tournament to free himself from unrequited love. He challenged all men of equal rank before they could cross the bridge, and is said to have broken 300 lances.

While the Knights Templar had a more concealed presence in this region, the Knights Hospitaller left their mark on Hospital de Órbigo. The Knights Hospitaller, officially known as the Order of the Hospital of Saint John of Jerusalem, originated in the early 12th century. Initially, they focused on offering medical care to pilgrims in Jerusalem. Over time, they evolved into a military order, providing armed escorts and defending the Holy Land. Their emblem, a white cross on a black background, became a symbol of their dual commitment to healing and defense. This cross is found all across Hospital de Órbigo.

Even though the Hospitallers and the Templars served the same purpose, they often didn't get along. There are many instances, especially in the Holy Land, where the two orders would battle each other. Another interesting fact is that after the Templars were disbanded throughout Europe, the Hospitallers inherited a large number of their properties. However, in Spain and Portugal, the Templar properties remained in Templar control for many years to come.

DAY 23:
HOSPITAL DE ÓRBIGO TO ASTORGA | 15.3 KM

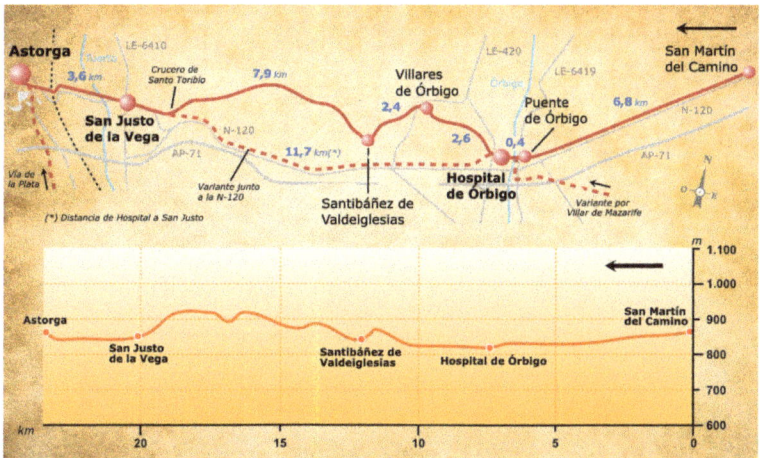

The next chapter in the Templars' mystery starts to unravel in Astorga. Known for its rich Roman heritage, Astorga was once a vital hub in the Roman gold trade, prominently positioned on the Via de la Plata. This ancient route, often referred to as the Silver Way, linked the north and south of the Iberian Peninsula, stretching from modern-day Seville to Astorga. The city's Roman roots are evident in its impressive architectural remnants, including the Roman walls that still stand guard over the old city.

Our search for the Templars on the Camino continues to Astorga's Cathedral, Santa Maria de Astorga. It is a centerpiece of religious and artistic heritage, housing treasures like the Lignum Crucis—this gold, jewel-encrusted relic contains a piece of the One True Cross. It is said that the relic was brought back from the Holy Land by the Knights Templar and housed at Ponferrada Castle before being moved to Astorga Cathedral.

DAY 24:
ASTORGA TO FONCEBADÓN |
28.5 KM

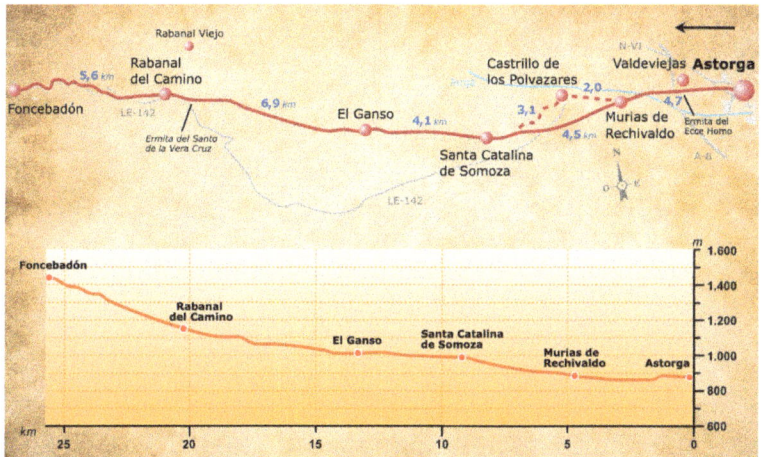

Leaving Astorga, it is a steady climb up to Foncebadon, one of the highest towns on the Camino. As you ascend the mountain, the air becomes fresh and the views are spectacular. Vast expanses of land open behind you and ahead majestic mountains touch the sky. Here, you also start to see signs of the Templars' legacy. The Camino markers on the trail also bear the Templars' Cross along with the yellow arrow, leading us both further on our Camino and closer to finding the Templars on the Camino.

In Rabanal del Camino, we know that some of the structures were built by the Templars, including a Templar house and barn, but why would they build here?

Looking back at the Game of the Goose, this section of the Camino lines up with the next Goose Square in the game. As we have discovered so far, where there is a goose, there is usually either spiritual or physical treasure to be found close by. It is the same here. Just a few kilometers away from Rabanal is Santa Colomba de Somoza. This location was once home to a Roman gold mine.

After you have explored a bit, I recommend continuing on to Foncebadón. Tomorrow is going to be a big day.

DAY 25:
FONCEBADÓN TO ESPINOSO
DE COMPLUDO | 22 KM

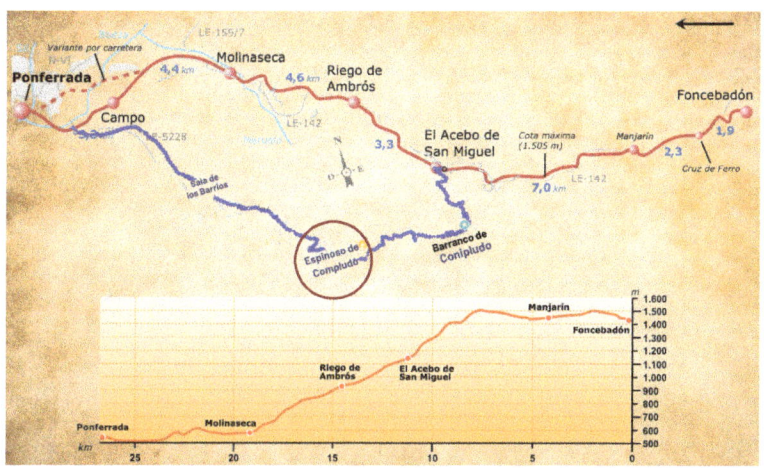

I am so excited for your journey today! I recommend that you wake up before the sun and walk the 1.9 km to Cruz de Ferro to catch the sunrise. Cruz de Ferro is the highest part of the Camino Frances. Here you will find a giant iron cross with a mound of stones at its base. It is a tradition for pilgrims to bring a stone from home and leave it at the base of the cross as a representation of a memory or loss that they would like to leave behind.

Continuing from here, another 2.3 km, you will reach Manjarin. Here, there is a small Templar hermitage that, up until recently, has been occupied by a Templar named Thomas. The alburge can sleep six people and doesn't have running water or electricity. If it is open, take a look around and feel like you are stepping back in time.

Next, we will deviate from the Camino for an adventure! 7 km from Manjarin is El Acebo de San Miguel. Here we will leave the Camino Frances and make our way to Espinoso de Compludo. In this small mountain town, lives the current Grand Master of the Knights Templar in Ponferrada. He runs a small tavern there called the Taberna Espinoso de Compludo. You won't be able to miss it. If you are fortunate enough, he will be there and will share some of the Templar legend and lore.

From El Acebo de San Miguel, it is around 10.2 km. About 3.7 km outside of El Acebo, you will find the Herrería de Compludo. This is the oldest blacksmith forge in Spain and is well worth a look. The whole forge is powered by a waterfall and is a feat of engineering. This forge is usually closed, but if you are lucky, the black smith will be there and the fires burning.

The ascent is steep on the way to Espinoso de Compludo, and the views are breathtaking. As you climb, we pass the spot of yet another Roman gold mine. Could this actually have been the mine connected to the Goose in the Game of the Goose? Inside Espinoso, there are three places to stay: La Casita de Chocolate, Las Cuatro Estaciones, and Casa de Juan. One last thing to check out in the town, carved into the wooden church door, we find the Seed of Life once more.

DAY 26:
ESPINOSO DE COMPLUDO TO PONFERRADA | 14.6 KM

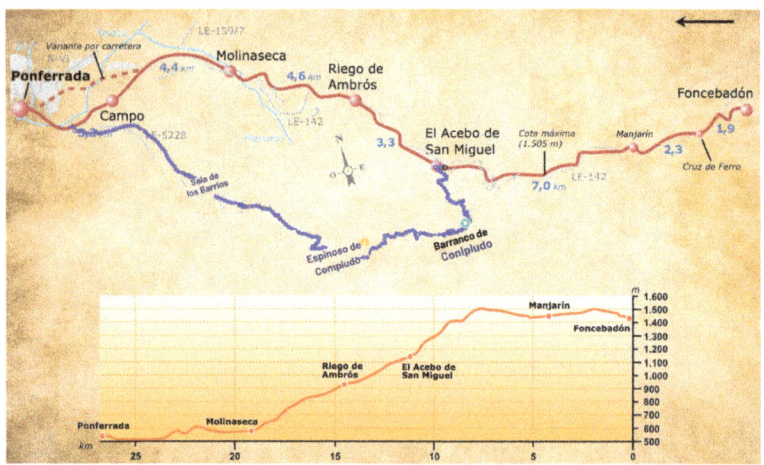

The trail from Espinoso to Ponferrada is off the traditional Camino, so you won't find markers. Make sure you are prepared with a map preloaded on your phone.

Reaching Ponferrada, we arrive at one of the greatest Templar sites in all of Europe—the Castillo de los Templarios, or Templars' Castle. This castle is one of the largest and best-preserved Templar sites in the world. At the beginning of July, the Asociación de Amigos de la Noche Templaria hosts the Noche Templaria (Templar Night), where the whole town comes together to celebrate its Templar heritage.

In 1177, the Templars received the ruins of a Roman fort, which became the castle in Ponferrada, situated in the heart of the Bierzo region, far from the looming threat of Muslim conquests. Originally known as Interamnium Flavium by the Romans, Ponferrada became a focal point for Templar activity. The Templars meticulously rebuilt the castle to unparalleled excellence—a true testament to their engineering skill.

Over time, the castle became a reliquary. Here, the Templars safeguarded holy relics, including the Lignum Crucis, which you saw in Astorga, and La Virgen de la Encina (Our Lady of the Oak). Today, you can see La Virgen de la Encina inside the Basílica de la Virgen de la Encina in Ponferrada. Legend has it that the black statue of the Virgin was carved by St. Luke and was brought to Spain. The statue was lost at one point in time. Then, during the construction of the castle, it was found inside an oak tree.

Another legend around the castle in Ponferrada is the legend of Jacques de Molay's missing sword. Legend has it that Molay traveled to Ponferrada while raising money for a new crusade to the Holy Land. It is said that he left his sword at the castle as a pledge that he would return.

In Ponferrada, we also find a connection to the Game of the Goose. Ponferrada lines up perfectly with space 42 on the Game of the Goose. This square is the Maze Square. When a player lands on this square, they must move back to space 30. It is a place that repels. What secret could the Templars be pushing others away from?

Two other interesting points about the castle itself: first, there is a Templar library inside. Here, you can actually look at historic books if you make a reservation. Second, over the main entrance is the Tau cross. We spoke about this earlier at the Arc of San Anton. Why would it be here? The answer lies in the Lemos family. After the Templars were disbanded everywhere else in Europe, the Templars continued on in Ponferrada for another sixty years. Eventually, though, the properties had to change hands, and Ponferrada Castle, along with several other Templar holdings, were given to the Lemos family, who were from Castrojeriz and associated with the Tau.

Ponferrada served as a hub for Templar operations, with the acquisition and construction of other castles cementing their dominance in the Bierzo region, including Cornatel, Corullon, Pieros, Tremor, Antares, and Balboa. But the question remains, why did the Templars choose this region?

DAY 27:
PONFERRADA TO LAS MÉDULAS | 27.8 KM

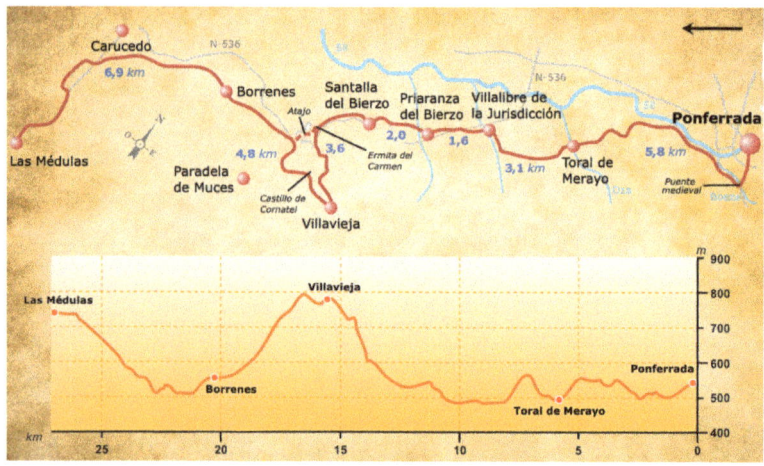

The answer to why the Templars were found here is the same reason why the Romans originally settled here—gold. The Templars capitalized on the proximity of Ponferrada to Las Médulas, the Romans' largest gold mine, which had been abandoned for centuries. This mine lies 27.8 km away from Ponferrada and is the first stop on the Camino Invierno, also known as the Winter Camino.

This Camino route leads from Ponferrada to Santiago in ten days. It is a great alternative to the traditional French Route. There are fewer people and some amazing things to see. This route was originally used by Roman legions and takes you through the valley of the River Sil. The elevation of this route is lower than the traditional route, making it a great option for pilgrims during the winter months.

The first stop of Templar interest on this route is the Castle of Cornatel. While there is still debate about the origins of the castle, it is believed to have been built originally by the Romans to protect the gold mine operations at Las Médulas. It is also said that this castle was one of the first donations made to the Templars. This castle is absolutely beautiful. Definitely leave yourself some time to explore and soak in the history.

As the day concludes, you reach Las Médulas. As stated before, this was the largest gold mine in the entire Roman Empire. They had a unique process of mining called the "devastation of the mountain." In it, they would bore holes into the mountain and pump massive amounts of water into it until the mountain crumbled. You can see the remains of this technique as you walk through the impressive canyon-like orange/red stone left behind.

When the Templars moved into this region, the mines had been abandoned for centuries. The Templars, known for their mining skills, could have easily rebooted these ancient mines and used the gold to help fund the construction of the cathedrals along the Camino.

Las Médulas also lines up perfectly with space 45 on the Game of the Goose, where the next Goose Square is found.

One last note, albergues in Las Médulas are pricier than other locations on the Camino. If you are on a budget, I would recommend stopping in one of the towns before.

KINGDOM OF

GALICIA

DAY 28:
LAS MÉDULAS TO O' BARCO DE VALDEORRAS | 27.2 KM

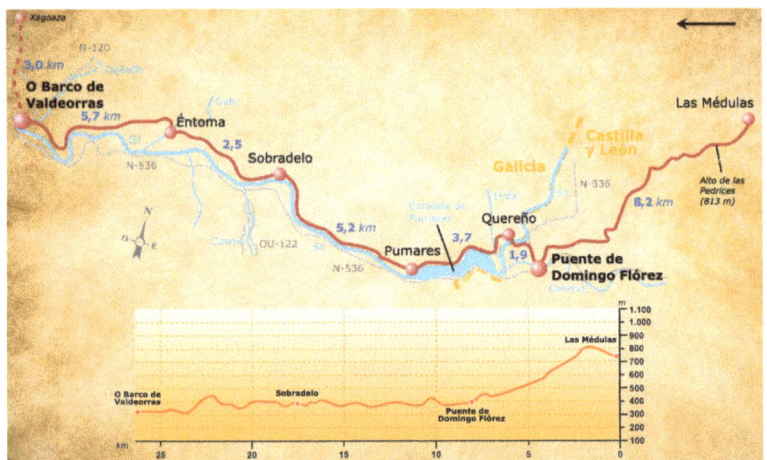

he descent from Las Médulas to Puente de Domingo Flórez takes you down about four hundred meters, intersecting with the Cabrera River in Puente de Domingo Flórez.

The Cabrera River is a tributary of the Sil River, which historically has had a high amount of gold in it. For years, prospectors known as aureanos have panned for gold here. Following the Templars on this Camino has been like a crime movie—all you have to do is follow the money.

As we cross the Sil River, we leave the Kingdom of León and enter the Kingdom of Galicia, a land rich in culture, legend, and spirituality. Just like all the Kingdoms in Spain, Galicia went through many changes over the years—below is a brief history.

The Roman Era
(25 BC - 476 AD)

Galicia's story begins long before the first pilgrims arrived. In 25 BC, the Romans conquered the Celtic Gallaeci people, integrating the region into the Roman Empire as the province of Gallaecia. Over the next several centuries, Roman influence brought infrastructure, towns, and roads to the area. Although the region was not a major economic center, its integration into the Roman Empire laid the foundations for the medieval world that would emerge.

The Roman era ended around 476 AD, following the fall of the Western Roman Empire. Galicia, like much of the Iberian Peninsula, would be shaped by the arrival of new cultures and powers in the ensuing centuries.

The Early Middle Ages
(409 - 711 AD)

The early Middle Ages saw the establishment of the Kingdom of the Suebi in 409 AD, after the Germanic tribe of the Suebi settled in the region. This was one of the first Germanic

99

kingdoms to form after the fall of the Roman Empire, and it lasted until 585 AD, when it was incorporated into the Visigothic Kingdom.

By the 8th century, the region became part of the Kingdom of Asturias following the Islamic conquests. Despite the Muslim invasions, Galicia largely remained in Christian hands and played an important role in the Reconquista, the gradual reconquest of the Iberian Peninsula.

THE HIGH MIDDLE AGES (9TH - 13TH CENTURY): THE RISE OF SANTIAGO

In the 9th century, a pivotal event took place that would change the course of history for Galicia—and indeed all of Spain. Around 813 AD, the tomb of St. James (Santiago) was discovered in the Libredon forest, near what is now Santiago de Compostela. According to legend, Bishop Theodemir of Iria Flavia recognized the tomb and marked the site, leading to the establishment of the Santiago de Compostela Cathedral.

St. James, one of Christ's twelve apostles, is believed to have preached in Galicia around 40 AD, spreading Christianity in the region. After his martyrdom in 44 AD, his body was said to have been miraculously transported back to Galicia, where it lay undisturbed for centuries. The discovery of his tomb sparked the creation of the Camino de Santiago, or Way of St. James, a pilgrimage route that would become one of the most important in Christendom. Pilgrims from across Europe began to travel to Santiago de Compostela, and the route soon grew into a symbol of faith and devotion. Today, you are continuing that tradition.

As we reach O Barco de Valdeorras, get plenty of rest and supplies. Tomorrow is going to be a big day.

DAY 29:
O Barco de Valdeorras to Quiroga | 38.5 KM

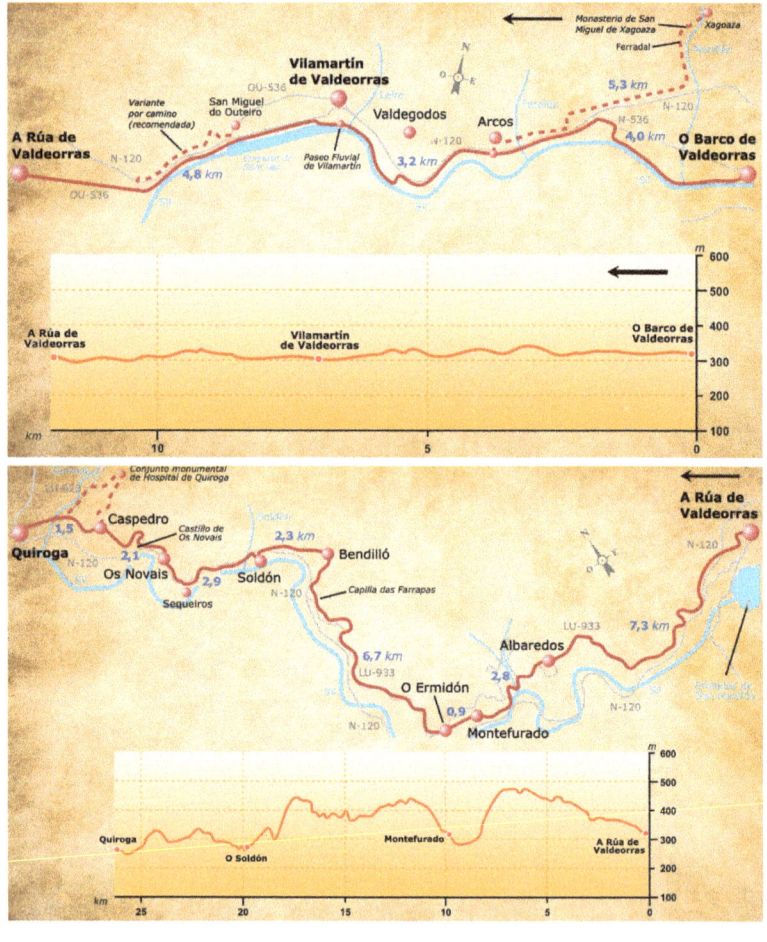

Today, we are combining two stages on the Camino: O Barco de Valdeorras to A Rúa de Valdeorras (12 km) and A Rúa de Valdeorras to Quiroga (26.5 km), making today's journey 38.5 km.

Along the journey, just outside of Montefurado, you will find the Montefurado Tunnel. The Camino passes above it, but I encourage you to go in for a closer look. Here, we discover another great feat of Roman engineering. This tunnel spans 120 meters and is over 20 meters high. The Romans constructed it to divert the entire Sil River to mine the rich gold bed that lay below.

At one point in time, there was a partial collapse of the tunnel, destroying the castle above. It is speculated that the castle was of Templar origin and that the Templars could have used the tunnel for another purpose.

The Montefurado Tunnel lines up perfectly with space 50 on the Game of the Goose. This space contains a Goose Square, linking it to the Templars. It is also rumored that there is a vast tunnel complex that stretches all the way from Ponferrada to Monforte de Lemos, which is about 35 km west on the Camino, and the vast tunnel of Montefurado lies in the middle.

Could the Templars have once again followed the Roman gold trail, using this tunnel as part of an underground network for transporting gold?

DAY 30:
QUIROGA TO MONFORTE DE LEMOS | 35.4 KM

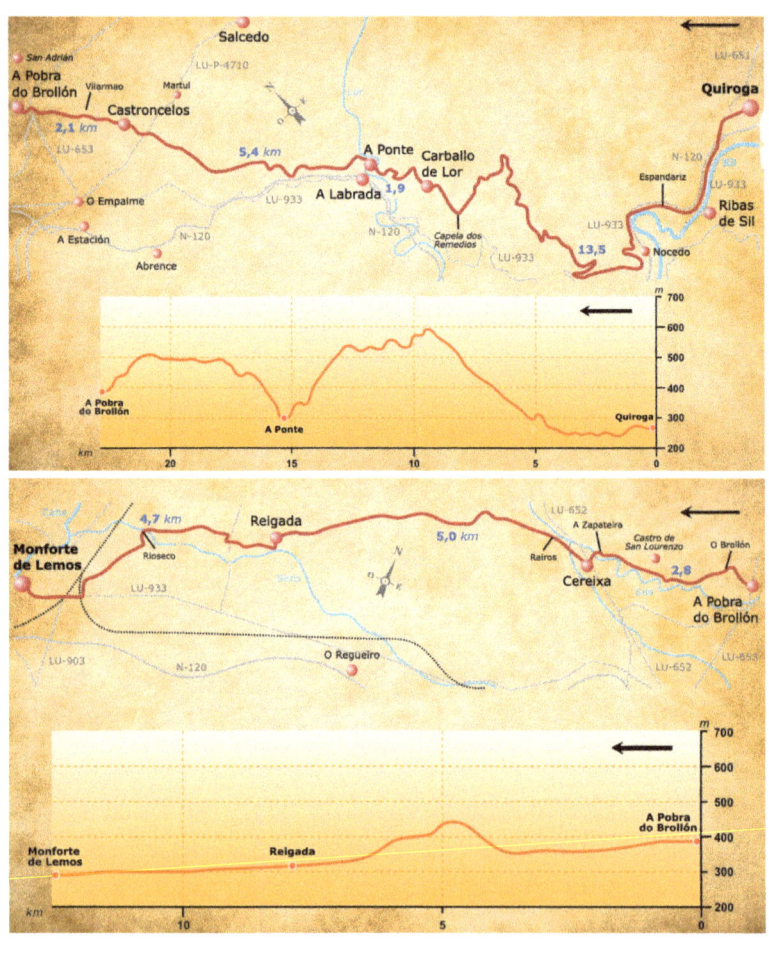

We are doubling up again today, walking from Quiroga to A Pobra do Brollón (22.9 km) and A Pobra do Brollón to Monforte de Lemos (12.5 km) for a total of 35.4 km.

Monforte de Lemos lines up perfectly with space 53 in the Game of the Goose. This square holds the dice in it, and here we find a connection which cannot be denied.

Monforte de Lemos Castle was constructed by the Lemos family, who originally came from the Castrojeriz area. The crest of the family is the six-sided dice. It has to be more than a coincidence that this square in the Game of the Goose has dice on it.

Another symbol associated with the family is the Tau, which is found on the Arc of San Anton as well as the front entrance to the castle of Ponferrada.

After the Templars were officially disbanded in other places in Europe, they continued strong for several years longer in this region of Spain. Eventually, though, the Templars and their possessions were absorbed into other military orders or passed on to families like the Lemos.

Inside the tower, we find more iconography associated with the Templars, including this chest, which contains both a Templar cross and a Seed of Life.

DAY 31:
Monfort de Lemos to Chantada | 30.4 km

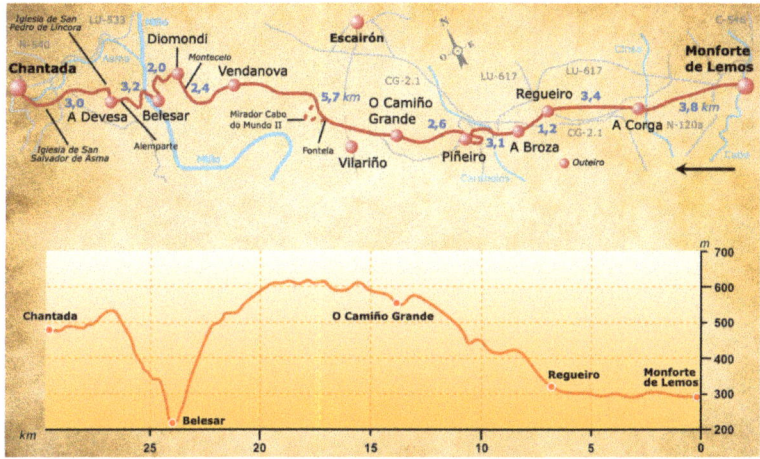

Today's walk brings us 30.4 km from Monforte de Lemos to Chantada and a possible split in the Templars' Camino.

25.2 km from Monforte de Lemos, the Camino crosses the Miño River at Belesar. This location lines up with space 54 on the Game of the Goose, and the river is also said to be a source of gold. More importantly, though, it flows all the way to the sea and separates Galicia from Portugal, which was a very Templar-friendly nation. It is easy to hypothesize that gold mined at Las Médulas could have been shipped down the Miño River to Portugal.

To sail from Belesar to the sea on the Miño River would take eight to twelve days. In the Game of the Goose, there are ten spaces from square 54, where Belesar is located, to the end of the game and winning. Also, on space 59, there is another goose. Halfway down the voyage, you get to Arbo, where there is another cluster of Templar sites.

It is easy to think that the Templars' path deviated from the Camino here toward Portugal, but we will talk about that in another book. Enjoy the last few days on the Camino de Santiago and let the miles you have walked sink in.

DAY 32:
CHANTADA TO RODERIO | 25.4 KM

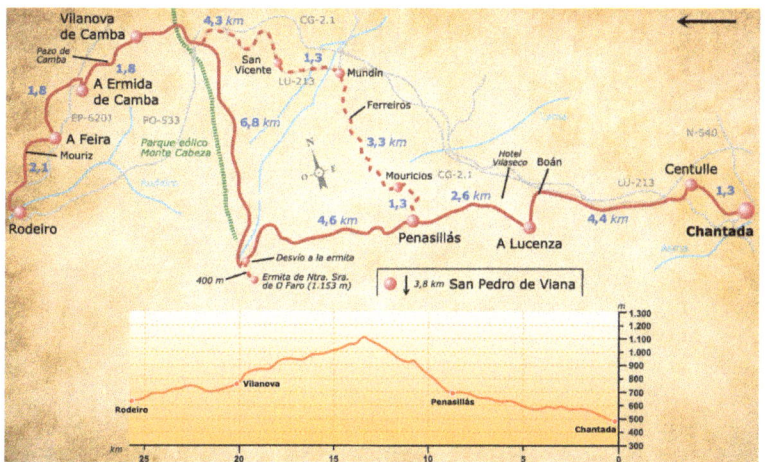

oday's journey takes us 25.4 km from Chantada to Rodeiro through the rolling green hills of Galicia. This stretch of the Camino is quiet and pastoral, allowing space for reflection. Today, we turn our thoughts to what became of the Templars' legacy after their suppression.

After the Templars were officially disbanded in 1312, their vast network of lands and holdings didn't simply disappear. In most of Europe, their properties were handed over to the Knights Hospitaller. But here in Spain, things unfolded differently. Many of the Templars' assets remained in Templar hands for years. Eventually, they were passed on to other military orders—including one that would rise to prominence in this region: the Knights of St. James.

The Knights of St. James, also known as the Order of Santiago, were founded in the 12th century with a dual mission: to protect pilgrims walking to Santiago de Compostela and to fight in the Reconquista. Unlike the Templars, whose roots stretched to Jerusalem, the Knights of St. James were born on the Iberian Peninsula and operated under the direct authority of the Spanish crown.

Their emblem—a red cross shaped like a sword placed on a scallop shell—was a symbol of both protection and war. In the centuries that followed, the Knights of St. James inherited many former Templar properties, converting commanderies and chapels once marked by the Templar cross to their own order.

DAY 33:
RODERIO TO SILLEDA | 37.6 KM

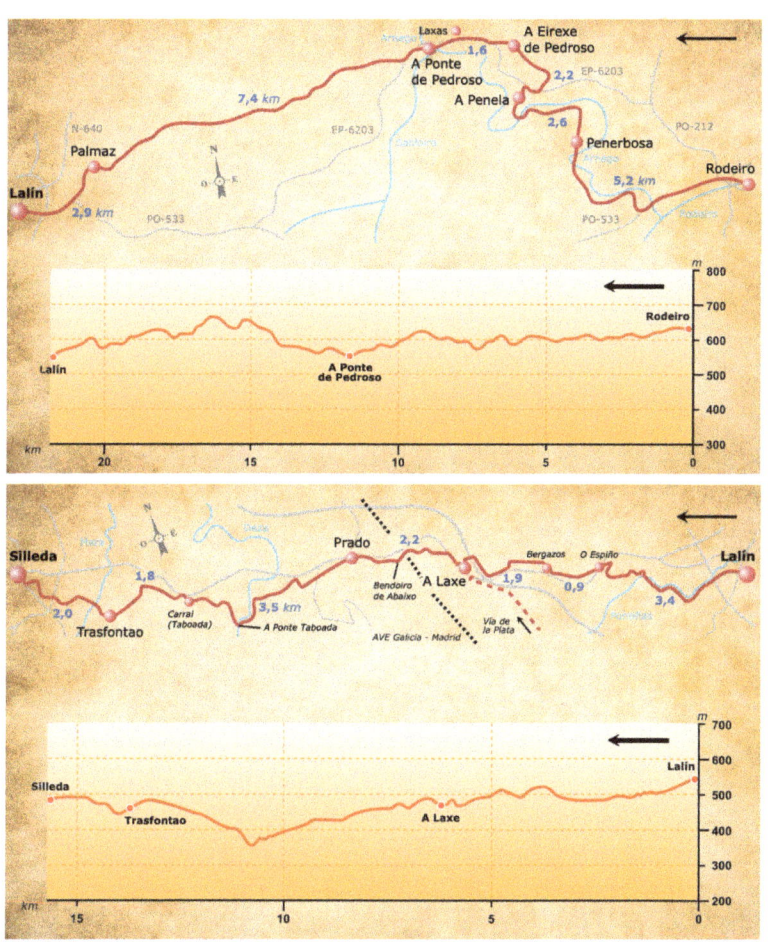

Today, we combine two stages of the Camino, walking 37.6 kilometers from Rodeiro to Silleda. This stretch marks the end of the Camino de Invierno. In Lalín, we merge with the Vía de la Plata, joining pilgrims who have walked all the way from the south of Spain.

The Winter Camino followed the most likely path of the Templars and also helps you to avoid the crowded last 100 km of the French Camino. It carried us through valleys and along rivers, past Roman tunnels and Templar legends. But here, the road shifts. From A Laxe onward, we walk with those on the Vía de la Plata—Spain's longest pilgrimage route.

The Vía de la Plata has deep roots. It follows an old Roman road that once connected Mérida in the south to Astorga in the north; we have talked about this in a previous chapter. Over time, this ancient trade route became a path for pilgrims—many of them Mozarabs, Christians living under Muslim rule—seeking Santiago. Like other Caminos, it soon became lined with monasteries, hospitals, and even Templar commanderies.

DAY 34:
SILLEDA TO SANTIAGO DE COMPOSTELA | 40.6 KM

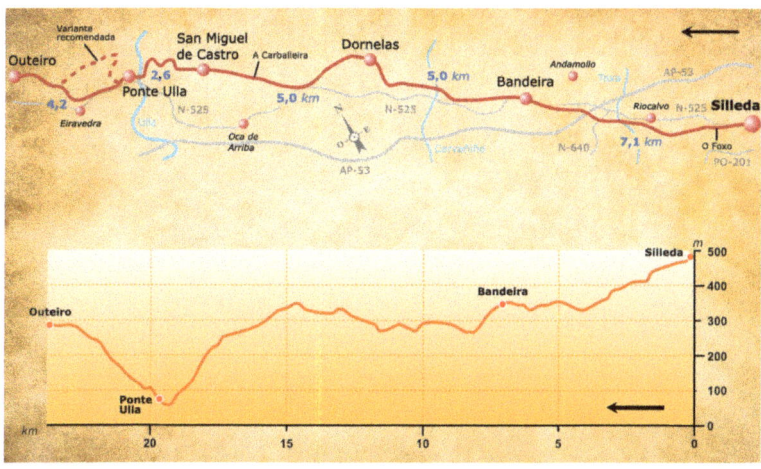

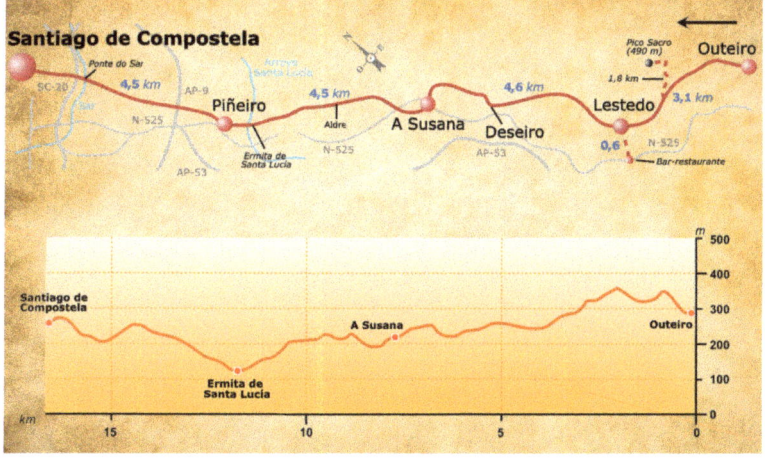

Today, we embark on the final leg of the Templars' Camino, traveling 40.6 kilometers from Silleda to Santiago de Compostela; the resting place of Saint James the Greater.

According to legend, St. James left Spain and returned to Jerusalem around 44 AD and was martyred. After his death, his disciples transported his remains by sea back to the Galician coast, landing at Padrón. From there, they carried his body inland to be buried in the forest of Libredón. Centuries later, in 813 AD, a hermit named Pelagius witnessed lights over a field, leading to the discovery of the apostle's tomb. This event prompted King Alfonso II of Asturias to commission the construction of a chapel on the site, marking the inception of Santiago de Compostela as a pilgrimage destination.

Arriving at the Cathedral in Santiago is a memory you will carry with you for your whole life. It is an indescribable feeling after walking all of those miles. Take a few minutes or hours in the square watching pilgrims reunite with their Camino families and take a moment to celebrate—you made it. After you let it all sink in, let's venture inside.

Inside the cathedral, there are so many things to be seen, but I want to talk about something that can't be seen anymore. The images below were sent to me by C. L. Morales. These photographs were taken of the central dome inside the cathedral. It is of the All-Seeing Eye, also known as the Eye of Providence, which is a symbol representing divine omniscience or the watchful eye of God. It is typically depicted as a single eye, often enclosed within a triangle and surrounded by rays of light. This iconography has roots in various cultures and religions, dating back to ancient civilizations. This symbol isn't directly related to the Templars but is associated with modern-day Freemasons. Up until 2010, this icon could be seen, but it has now been replaced. It leaves us to question what else has been covered up on the Camino, and also shows the importance of researching and documenting what we can when it is still there.

After you visit the cathedral, I recommend that you visit the Pilgrims' Museum, where you will find an original copy of the Codex Calixtinus, a 12th-century manuscript that played a pivotal role in shaping the Camino de Santiago. Often considered the first travel guide, this codex offered pilgrims sermons, liturgical texts, miracle stories, and practical advice for the journey to the shrine of Saint James.

The codex is attributed to Pope Calixtus II, but was likely compiled by the French cleric Aymeric Picaud around 1140. However, the deeper story lies in its political and familial roots. Before ascending to the papacy, Calixtus was Guy of Burgundy, the younger brother of Raymond of Burgundy, who ruled Galicia in the late 11th century. Raymond married Urraca of León and Castile, daughter of Alfonso VI, and governed this region during a crucial time in the growth of the pilgrimage. It is easy to draw a connection between the book being written to increase the number of pilgrims and these family ties, even though Raymond died in 1107.

Interestingly, the Urraca married to Raymond of Burgundy was the same Urraca from the earlier legend of the Holy Grail in León, and in her second marriage, Urraca married Alfonso the Battler, King of Aragon, though it was an unhappy union. It is also believed that Urraca gave the Templars properties and land, and in turn, they backed her as a ruler. At one time, she was named the Empress of all of Spain. She is the thread that ties the beginning of your pilgrimage together with the end, and her sister, Theresa, Countess of Portugal, ties us into your next adventure on the Portuguese Camino.

OTHER BOOKS
BY BRIAN JOHN SKILLEN ABOUT
THE CAMINO DE SANTIAGO

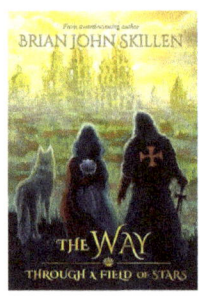

The Way: Through a Field of Stars

There is a secret code of the Knights Templar on the Camino de Santiago... *The Way: Through a Field of Stars* is the first book in a sweeping historical fantasy trilogy set on the Camino de Santiago one year before the Templars disappeared along with their treasure.

Back: Through a Field of Stars

Hunted by the seven deadly sins, two unlikely heroes must deliver a secret message across the Camino de Santiago before it's too late...

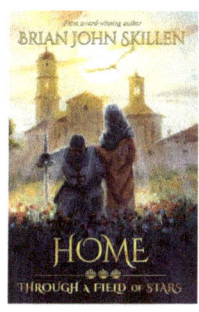

Home: Through a Field of Stars

Find The Way Back Home as you un-cover the secret treasure of the Knights Templar on the Camino de Santiago… Enjoy the exciting conclusion to the Through a Field of Stars trilogy as you uncover the secrets the Templars left behind.

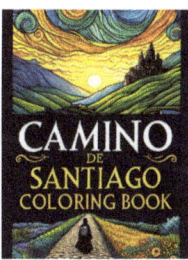

The Camino de Santiago Coloring Book

Take a virtual pilgrimage on the Cami-no de Santiago with the Camino de Santiago Coloring book!

Use this link to learn more about Brian and his books!

https://linktr.ee/brianjohnskillen

BIBLIOGRAPHY

Atienza, Juan García. *The Knights Templar in the Golden Age of Spain*. Rochester, VT: Inner Traditions, 2006.

Lalanda, Fernando. *El juego templario de la oca en el Camino de Santiago*, 2013.

Nicholson, Helen. *The Knights Templar: A New History*. Stroud, UK: Sutton Publishing, 2001.

Silva, Freddy. *The First Templar Nation: How Eleven Knights Created a New Country and a Refuge for the Grail*. Rochester, VT: Destiny Books, 2017.

Oldenbourg, Zoé. *The Crusades*. Translated by Peter Green. New York: Pantheon Books, 1966.

ABOUT THE AUTHOR

Author Brian John Skillen believes we are all called to adventure. Whether we answer this call by traveling around the world or by living vicariously through our favorite characters—we are born to explore.

In all of his adventures around the world, nothing has affected him more than his pilgrimages along the Camino de Santiago. It was here that he was first told about a secret code of the Knights Templar on the Camino. This code inspired him to write the Through a Field of Stars series as well as this guidebook. Since his first pilgrimage in 2017, he has walked over 1,500 miles across Spain doing research for his books.

He has traveled the miles that his characters have traveled and learned the lessons they have learned. He writes in the hopes that his books will inspire you to have a life-changing adventure on the Camino de Santiago.

 Use this link to learn more about Brian and his books! https://linktr.ee/brianjohnskillen

P.S. Reviews are the lifeblood of independent authors. If you enjoyed this book, please consider leaving us a review wherever you purchased it. Also, let me be the first to wish you a Buen Camino!

www.ingramcontent.com/pod-product-compliance
Lightning Source LLC
Chambersburg PA
CBHW051213120626
46547CB00013B/1327